Understanding Children

Dr Richard Woolfson is a child psychologist, working with troubled children and their families, and is a Fellow of the British Psychological Society. He is a regular contributor to *Nursery World* and *Who Minds?*, as well as to other popular magazines including *Practical Parenting* and *Right Start*. Richard is the author of several popular books on child psychology, and also appears regularly on radio and television. He is married to a child psychologist; they have two children.

Other Books By The Same Author

AN A–Z OF CHILD DEVELOPMENT
Published by Souvenir Press.

CHILDREN WITH SPECIAL NEEDS
Published by Faber & Faber.

STARTING SCHOOL
To be published by Thorsons, in 1995

Understanding Children

A Guide For Parents & Carers

DR RICHARD C. WOOLFSON

Caring Books: Glasgow

First published in 1989, by Faber and Faber
Reprinted in 1990.
Published in Italian in 1993, by Franco Angeli
Republished 1994, and only available from
Caring Books, PO Box 1565, Glasgow G46 6SX.

Printed and bound in Great Britain by Ipswich Book Company.

All rights reserved.

British Library Cataloguing in Publication Data.

© Richard C. Woolfson, 1994

Richard Woolfson asserts the moral right to be identified as the author of this work.

This book is sold subject to the condition that it shall not,
by way of trade or otherwise, be lent, resold, hired out
or otherwise circulated without the publisher's prior consent
in any form of binding or cover other than that in which
it is published and without a similar condition including this
condition being imposed on the subsequent purchaser.

ISBN 0-9523649-0-5

to Tessa and Eve

Contents

Acknowledgements ix
Introduction – A Guide for Parents and Carers 1
1. Nature versus Nurture in Child Development 3
2. Personality Development 9
3. Is My Child's Behaviour Normal, or is She Disturbed? 20
4. Attention 31
5. Comforters 43
6. Aggression 50
7. Jealousy 57
8. Fears in Childhood 65
9. Birth Order and Personality 73
10. Shyness 84
11. Separation and Divorce 91
12. Remarriage and Step-Parenting 99
13. Independence 106
14. Self-Image 116
15. Language Development 126
16. Stealing, Lying and Swearing 138
17. Socialization 148
18. Discipline 159
19. Children with Special Needs 167
Developmental Checklists 176.
Index 210

Acknowledgements

Thanks to Lisa, Tessa and Eve for their love, support and encouragement.

Introduction

A Guide for Parents and Carers

Becoming involved in the care, education and development of young children is a huge responsibility – and it doesn't matter whether you are involved as a parent, a nursery nurse, a childminder, a health visitor, or any other childcare professional. You want to 'get it right' during the pre-school years, so that the child grows to be happy, confident, capable and fulfilled.

Yet there is no one 'right' way to bring up and develop children. Being with young children – as parent or childcare professional – means you have to be flexible, and this theme is reinforced throughout *Understanding Children*. True, there are many principles of child-rearing that apply to everyone. But in many cases, what suits you may not suit someone else. This book will not provide you with specific answers to your specific questions. It will not tell you what to do every time you have a problem with children. What it will do, however, is provide you with an understanding of the growing emotional and psychological needs of young children, and how you can influence their development.

The structure of *Understanding Children*

This book is written for parents and for a variety of professionals involved in children's care, education and development. Therefore, the phrase 'your child' is used frequently, and refers to any child you are involved with either as a parent or as a carer.

Understanding Children

The first three chapters look at genetic and environmental influences on development in childhood, with particular reference to personality development. Opposing psychological theories are discussed and consideration is given to the difference between normality and abnormality in childhood. These introductory chapters provide you with a perspective for understanding the remainder of the book.

Subsequent chapters are directed at specific areas of child psychology that are of concern to anyone involved with children. The book concludes with a section on the main developmental changes in the pre-school years, in the form of checklists that cover physical, emotional, social, intellectual and linguistic milestones.

Chapter 1

Nature versus Nurture in Child Development

Children come in all sorts of shapes, sizes, abilities and personalities. But what makes one child different from another? Is 'nature' (the child's inborn inherited characteristics) more important than 'nurture' (the child's characteristics as a result of environmental influences). Some people take an extreme view. John Locke argued that the mind of a newborn baby is a blank slate (*tabula rasa*) and that the slate becomes filled as a result of the baby's experiences in life. He believed a child's development has nothing to do with any characteristics she inherits from her parents, and instead entirely depends on her experiences in childhood. Another philosopher, Rousseau, took the opposite view. He believed a child has all her characteristics by the time she is born and that if she is allowed to develop naturally, without any outside interference, then she will grow into a mature, moral and knowledgeable adult.

Both these extreme views are wrong. Careful research has shown that child development is a combination of the inherited features and the influence of the environment. Both 'nature' factors and 'nurture' factors interact to affect the growing child.

Genetic influences at conception

Inherited attributes are transmitted from parents to child at the time of conception. Every human body is made up of millions of tiny cells and usually each cell contains twenty-three pairs of chromosomes (those parts of the cell that have the blueprint for the growth and development of the body). Two of these chromosomes are sex chromosomes, while the remainder are responsible for other characteristics. In male cells, one of the sex chromosomes is X and the other is Y, while in female cells both sex chromosomes are X. Sperm cells have only twenty-three chromosomes, with only one sex chromosome, and this may be either an X or a Y. Female egg cells also have only twenty-three chromosomes but the sex chromosome will always be an X. At fertilization, if the sperm cell has an X-chromosome then a girl will be produced (XX). If the sperm cell contains a Y-chromosome then a boy will be produced (XY).

Once the sperm cell has fertilized the egg, the developing foetus has forty-six chromosomes (in twenty-three pairs), half of which are exact duplicates of the mother's chromosomes and half of which are exact duplicates of the father's chromosomes. So 50 per cent of the baby's genetic pre-programming comes from each parent. However, recent genetic research has found that at this stage a third element comes into play. Some pairs of chromosomes can break and then recombine to form new pairs – in combinations not found in either parent. In this way each individual has a genetic structure which, although it is formed from the ingredients of the parents' genetic input, is unique. Geneticists, therefore, now take the view that a child inherits only some of her parents' characteristics.

Each chromosome has thousands of smaller particles (genes) which carry instructions for physical development. The genes determine the child's sex, the size of the body, the colour of the eyes, skin and hair, the blood group, and so on. Genes interact to form complementary pairs, but some genes are 'dominant' (their instructions are recognized by the body in preference to the other gene in the pair) and some genes are 'recessive' (their instructions are not recognized by the body unless both genes in the pair are recessive). For example, the gene responsible for brown eyes is dominant and the gene responsible for blue eyes is recessive. At conception if the gene pair has two 'brown' genes, or has one of each colour, then the child will have brown eyes. On the other hand, if the gene pair has two 'blue' genes then the child will have blue eyes. In this way, it is possible for two brown-eyed parents to have a blue-eyed child (having inherited a recessive 'blue' gene from each parent), but it is not possible for two blue-eyed parents to have a brown-eyed child (since if either parent had a dominant 'brown' gene then they themselves would not be blue-eyed).

The way that genes act depends on the characteristics they control. While certain genes show their effect in early life, such as blood type and skin growth, others act only at specific periods in the child's development. These age-linked genes contain plans for sequences of events, such as the age teeth will appear in the child's mouth, when the child will talk, when menstruation will begin, and so on. There is no evidence, however, that genes carry plans for personality development.

Inherited malformations

The natural forces of development are such that a malformed foetus is usually aborted spontaneously early on in pregnancy. Over 95 per cent of all babies are born normal, with no defect whatsoever. Of those babies born with an abnormality, a small number have inherited the disorder from their parents, because either one or both parents carry the abnormal gene.

If the abnormal gene is dominant, then the parent who carries it will be affected by the abnormality. Even when the other parent is normal, any children born have a 50–50 chance of being affected. Dwarfism is an example of this. If the abnormal gene is recessive, the parents may not know they are carriers of the disorder because they themselves will have developed normally. Statistically, where two parents carry recessive abnormal genes, one in four of their children will have the disorder, half their children will be carriers, and one in four of the children will be completely unaffected. Cystic fibrosis – a disease in which the body glands produce too much mucus – is an example of recessive inherited disorder, which affects approximately two children in every thousand.

Influences on the foetus

Plans for development are laid down in the child's genetic blueprint at conception. But realization of this genetic potential is dependent on extraneous factors. Even before birth, foetal development is subject to environmental influences, some of which are physical and some psychological.

Physical influences are wide ranging. Research findings confirm that women who smoke twenty or more cigarettes daily during pregnancy have smaller and lighter babies than those women who do not smoke. Smoking in pregnancy increases the chance of having a still birth or a baby with some kind of malformation. There are psychological effects as well, which can be long-lasting. One study has shown that seven years after birth, children of mothers who smoked during their pregnancy were less able readers than children of non-smokers, and were more likely to be hyperactive. The developing foetus can also be affected by drugs taken by the mother. We live in a drug-taking society, in which the pharmaceutical industry persuades us to take its products for every minor ailment. It is difficult to break the habit during pregnancy, especially since many drugs are regarded as safe. But it is better to err on the side of caution. Some drugs marketed specifically for pregnant women have been found later to have serious side-effects. The tragedy of thalidomide is one such example of later child development being impaired through drugs affecting the foetus.

Similarly, foetal alcohol syndrome is a recognized condition found in children born of alcoholic mothers. The characteristics are small body weight, smaller brain size, mild to moderate developmental difficulties, and poor physical co-ordination. The excessive intake of alcohol during the

Nature versus Nurture in Child Development

mother's pregnancy places severe limitations on the child's actual development, despite a healthy genetic potential. Even the mother's diet during pregnancy influences foetal progress. Evidence from studies throughout the world confirms that severe malnutrition during pregnancy can increase the likelihood of still birth, low birth weight and baby deaths during the first year. Malnutrition appears to be more damaging when it occurs in the latter half of the pregnancy, especially in the final three months. Children born under these conditions have restricted development.

Disease during pregnancy is yet another developmental hazard. Although most diseases contracted by the mother while she is pregnant cannot be passed to the foetus through the placenta, there are a few exceptions, such as rubella (German measles). The risk of foetal damage is greater if the mother contracts the disease within the first twelve weeks of pregnancy. Rubella tends to impair the development of the eyes, ears and heart, and many affected children are born deaf. Fortunately, rubella is preventable through immunization before pregnancy.

Psychological influences on foetal development are equally diverse. The mother's emotional well-being during pregnancy affects the foetus, even though there is no direct connection between their nervous systems. As early as the 1940s, scientists were able to show that the mother's emotional condition during pregnancy can have a direct influence on foetal physiology. Emotional arousal in the pregnant woman causes a physical reaction that releases hormones into her bloodstream, and these chemical changes can irritate the foetus. Researchers have also found that foetal movements in the womb increase many times when the mother experiences emotional stress. Another study showed mothers of babies who had colic had been more tense during their pregnancy compared to mothers of babies who did not have colic.

Medical evidence confirms that a woman experiencing prolonged and severe psychological stress during pregnancy has an increased probability of having a premature delivery, a longer or more complicated labour, a miscarriage and a more difficult pregnancy. And the reason for the severe and prolonged stress doesn't matter. The effects appear to be the same. A stress-free pregnancy is the ideal, though not always possible.

Influences on the child

After birth, the child's development remains subject to the influences of extraneous factors. Physically, a baby must be able to satisfy her basic needs of hunger, thirst and shelter if she is to survive, let alone achieve full potential. But there are also psychological needs that must be met in order for the baby to thrive. Most importantly, a child needs love and attention from a caring parent (or parent substitute) in the pre-school years. Failure to have at least one close emotional connection with an adult can result in social difficulties in later life. A child also has a need for structure and consistency provided by a stable family life. Removal of this can leave the child with feelings of insecurity and anxiety. The many different areas of child development affected by parent-child relationships are discussed in the remaining chapters of this book.

Chapter 2

Personality Development

Having considered child development in general in the previous section, let's now consider personality development in particular – because the manner in which a child behaves, the way he relates to his parents, the way he interacts with his friends and how he copes with stress, all affect his contentment throughout life. When psychologists talk of 'personality', they use the term differently from the way it is used in everyday language. You may describe someone as having 'bags of personality' because he is very lively, talkative, the life-and-soul of the party, has a good sense of humour and is outgoing. Similarly, you may describe someone as having 'no personality' because he is quiet and withdrawn from other people, likes to keep himself to himself, and avoids social encounters wherever possible. Psychologists, however, use the word 'personality' in a broader sense to indicate all the emotional and behavioral attributes which combine to form a unique individual. Everybody has personality, whether they are quiet or talkative, confident or insecure, sociable or solitary. Right from birth, a baby shows that it has a personality of its own and responds to its mother and father in a unique way.

Genetic influences on personality development

There is little evidence to suggest the genes carry a blueprint for personality development in the way they do for other areas of development, though there have been many attempts to demonstrate this. Francis Galton, an eighteenth-century British psychologist, believed that all individual differences between people are due to inherited influences, and spent many years collecting evidence to support this view. He studied family histories, in the hope of showing that characteristics run in families, that generation after generation would share the same qualities. Although Galton did find that members of certain families were similar to those of preceding generations, there were always members who did not follow the predicted pattern. This suggested personality development was a blend of genetic and environmental influences. Galton's theory could not be substantiated.

The study of identical twins is regarded as the best way to examine the importance of genetic factors in personality development. When identical twins are conceived, a single egg that has already been fertilized by a sperm separates into two identical parts. Each part develops into a foetus. Since each baby comes from one egg (monozygotic), these twins are always of the same sex, with the same inherited genetic characteristics. (When non-identical twins are conceived, two entirely separate eggs are fertilized by separate sperm at the same time. Since each baby comes from a different egg – dizygotic – they are no more alike than any brother and sister.) If personality is entirely inherited then identical twins would always have identical personalities. But they do not. Parents of identical twins report that while there are similarities in temperament each twin develops his own unique and distinctive characteristics, again suggesting the importance of the environment in personality formation.

Physical influences on personality development

Hippocrates, the Greek philosopher, believed that personality is determined by the presence of one of four body fluids; yellow bile, black bile, blood and phlegm. Scientific progress has proved him wrong. Yet even today some people think there is a link between physical characteristics and personality. For example, there is the saying 'all red-haired people are bad-tempered'.

Phrenologists took the view that different parts of the brain are responsible for different aspects of human behaviour (we now know this is accurate to a certain extent) and that the outline of the skull at each part of the brain indicates how well developed that particular behaviour is (we now know this is inaccurate). A British doctor, Braid, was completely committed to phrenology. He claimed that by depressing selected bumps on a patient's head, the patient would behave in new and predictable ways. The control of personality, however, is not that simple and Braid's theories quickly floundered along with the rest of phrenology.

In 1925, E. Kretschmer, a German doctor, argued that personality is directly related to an individual's body size and body shape. He classified body types into four categories; pyknic (short and plump), asthenic (tall and slim), athletic (well-proportioned) and dysplastic (misshapen). Each type was thought to lead to a distinct personality, for instance, the typical pyknic is described as sociable and outgoing, while the typical asthenic is described as quiet and serious. Developing this line of research, W. H. Sheldon photographed over 4,000 nude males from the front, side and back. Unlike E. Kretschmer (who argued for distinct body types) Sheldon argued there are three main components of body structure which combine in various ways to form the final body shape. Each component carried its own personality – the mixture of components accounting for the actual individual personality. For instance, endomorphy (roundedness and soft muscle tone) was thought to be linked to joviality, and mesomorphy (muscularity) to aggression and vigour. Scientific evidence does not support theories of this nature.

Even where people of specific body types behave in predicted ways, it is impossible to know whether the body type causes the personality or whether social expectations cause the personality. Parents who expect their red-haired child to be bad-tempered might behave in certain ways that confirm that view. They might interpret silence as sulkiness (not concentration), fussiness as irritability, and they might over-react every time he does lose his temper. Physical characteristics and social expectations merge together.

Personality development – the psychoanalytic perspective

Freud believed that childhood experiences are the greatest influence on personality development and that what happens in childhood continues to affect the individual throughout adulthood. His psychoanalytic theory regarded personality development as a combination of heredity and environment. Freud claimed that a child is born with a number of instincts, such as hunger, thirst, love, aggression and self-satisfaction. In the first five years of life, as parent–child relationships become firmly established, a child learns to control his instincts. Many of them become repressed into the unconscious, where they lie dormant for varying lengths of time. Freud looked on childhood as a period in which parents transform their baby from a primitive selfish creature into a sociable, disciplined member of society.

He proposed further that a child is affected by thoughts and feelings from two sources. First, there are conscious feelings of which he is aware, such as happiness, fear and confidence. And second, there are unconscious feelings of which he is not aware. Aside from containing unacceptable instinctive impulses, which are repressed by child-rearing practices, the unconscious also contains any unpleasant emotions that would cause the child distress if he was made aware of them. The unconscious is a dumping-ground for feelings that the child cannot accept. At some point, however, these unconscious feelings may begin to break through into consciousness in an uncontrolled way and cause the child to behave in a disturbed manner. This frequently happens when the child is under stress.

Both conscious and unconscious emotions affect the child as he grows up, though the unconscious has the greater effect. Freud argued that even the very trivial aspects of everyday behaviour, such as slips of the tongue, and mistakes when writing, are caused by unconscious feelings. He also claimed that jokes allow children and adults to release unconscious feelings harmlessly, and that is why they laugh. Therefore, he was the first to propose that what parents can directly observe in their children (behaviour) is caused by what they cannot directly observe (the unconscious).

Freud never worked with emotionally disturbed children – all his patients were disturbed adults. Led by Freud's daughter, Anna, later psychoanalysts developed play therapy, which rests on the assumption that play is a child's most natural form of communication. While adults are able to express themselves verbally, children are not as sophisticated in their use of language. Play lets the child express his true feelings, argue psychoanalysts, and that if he plays for long enough he will begin to release his deep-rooted unconscious emotions. Play therapy usually takes place in a large playroom with lots of toys, including a doll's house, art materials, modelling clay and puppets. The child is permitted to play with whatever toy he wants, while the psychoanalyst observes what he does with them. Through detailed interpretation of a child's behaviour in this situation, the psychoanalyst builds a picture of his unconscious feelings.

Psychoanalytic theory, as first outlined by Freud, has been modified over the years. Many of Freud's original ideas on child development have been rejected, largely because there is little scientific evidence to support some of his very extreme views. Yet certain aspects of his theory do remain, and many psychologists adopt a perspective on childhood which owes much to psychoanalysis. First, Freud's emphasis on the impact of parent–child relationships is widely accepted. Research has shown that a child deprived of love will fail to thrive psychologically. The first few years of life are very important in this respect. Children who fail to form a loving relationship with at least one adult before reaching the age of three often have personal difficulties in forming relationships throughout their whole lives. Satisfactory emotional attachments in early life are crucial for later personality development. Second, his concept that a child's observable behaviour can be influenced by unconscious feelings, his concept that unpleasant emotions are repressed into the unconscious, and his concept that disturbed behaviour in childhood can be caused by unconscious feelings are used by many contemporary psychologists. In the subsequent chapters of this book, which look at many different areas of child development, you will find this link between behaviour and unconscious emotions referred to many times.

Personality development – behaviourism

In the same way that psychoanalysis recognizes the impact of parents on their child's development, behaviourism – another dominant theory of child development – also sees parent–child relationships as being of prime importance. But for entirely different reasons. Behaviourism is concerned only with what we can see, namely, behaviour, and not with any thoughts or feelings that might underlie this behaviour. Furthermore, behaviourism argues that all behaviour is learned; nothing is inherited.

Nearly a hundred years ago, a Russian psychologist, Pavlov, showed that a dog could be trained to salivate to a stimulus other than food. By letting the dog hear the sound of a bell a few seconds before giving him a plate of food, Pavlov found that the dog soon learned to salivate as soon as he heard the bell, without the food even being present. In other words, the dog had been conditioned into new behaviour. One of Pavlov's students demonstrated that a young baby could be taught to salivate to a bell, just as the dog had been. The possibilities were endless. The reasoning of behaviourism ran as follows: if a psychologist can train an uncooperative primitive dog to behave in specific ways, then surely parents can teach their child to behave in whatever way they want.

Some years later, J. B. Watson – one of the first psychologists to develop behaviourism – took these theories one stage further. Arguing that a child has no inherited behaviour and that everything is learned from the environment, he

Personality Development

rejected any ideas about instincts and the unconscious. Watson claimed that what matters in child development is the way the parents mould their child's behaviour. For him, love and warmth are not necessary and, indeed, their presence could impair the child's progress. He advised parents against kissing and cuddling young babies, saying this would only reduce their ability to cope with life later on. However, this rather depressing view may well be a reflection of Watson's own unhappy childhood. In his autobiography, he was able to recall only a few pleasant incidents in childhood.

B. F. Skinner followed the behaviourist tradition that Watson had established. Using rats and other animals in many different laboratory experiments, he found that learning depends on how often the learner is rewarded and what he is rewarded with. He developed what he called 'laws of learning' – a system of axioms governing the way learning occurs. These laws of learning have led to some remarkable demonstrations. Using techniques of reward and punishment, Skinner was able to teach two pigeons to play table tennis with each other (the bats were suspended in front of the pigeons, who were taught to strike them with their beaks at the right moment, thereby returning the ball over the net to the opponent), and he taught rats how to run through mazes without making mistakes.

Extrapolating from animals to humans – a jump that many psychologists feel is invalid – Skinner proposed that a child can also be conditioned to learn anything in the same way that animals can, as long as the teaching process is broken down into small stages with each successive stage coming closer to the desired goal, and as long as there are ample rewards to reinforce each stage of the child's progress. The blend of rewarding a child when he behaves acceptably and punishing a child when he behaves unacceptably is the keynote of Skinner's behaviourism. Classroom teachers have been able to institute programmes of systematic reinforcement to encourage misbehaving pupils to conform. At no time did Skinner consider the effect a child's emotions might have on his behaviour.

Many psychologists reject behaviourism because it is so unconcerned with feelings. There are many aspects of child behaviour that are due to underlying emotions. A child on his own who cries because he loses his football behaves that way due to his feelings of sadness, not because he has been conditioned to cry. Furthermore, parents may find that when their child's misbehaviour has been eased by the application of behavioural methods, the child then misbehaves in a new way – one explanation being that the child's feelings are the root of the misbehaviour and these have not been dealt with. Second, a child may learn to behave appropriately when rewards and punishments are in force, but may resort to his previous misbehaviour once they have been withdrawn. The effects of behaviourism in practice are not long-lasting. A third reason for rejecting behaviourism is its assumption that a child is simply a reflection of – not an interaction with – his upbringing. The child is regarded as a passive being, there to be moulded by the influences of family life.

Despite its weaknesses, behaviourism has components which are employed by many psychologists today. In particular, the notions that parents can teach their child how to behave, that parents can inadvertently teach their child how to misbehave, and that the prudent use of rewards and punishment can have an effect on child development, are used by many contemporary psychologists.

Personality development – situationism

A third aspect that has to be considered when understanding personality development is the effect of the situation in which the child functions. 'Situationist' psychologists claim that a child's personality constantly changes as his immediate environment changes, and that there is no such thing as an enduring personality characteristic. They claim that children are not consistent in their personality from one situation to another.

The earliest research into this view of personality began in 1928 with a study investigating the differing levels of honesty that a child shows under different circumstances. Children in the study were tested in a number of situations where there was the possibility of being dishonest. For instance, each child in the project was taken into a room, left there and allowed to play with boxes containing money. The child did not know that every box had been secretly marked so that the researchers knew how much cash was in each one. This meant the child was in a situation where there was great temptation to steal, but where he thought there was no chance of being caught. Other experimental situations testing the child's honesty were the opportunity to cheat at school exams, and the chance to falsify academic records. The researchers found that honesty – a typical personality characteristic – varied as a child moved from situation to situation. No child was totally dishonest all the time, only a few were completely honest all the time, and virtually all the children that participated in the project cheated some of the time. The researchers concluded personality is situation-specific, not fixed.

Subsequent studies confirmed the apparently changeable nature of a child's personality as he moves from one environment to the next. However, much of this theory has been challenged on the grounds that it simply states the obvious. After all, everyone knows that a child behaves differently when, say, he is being given a telling-off from his teacher for not doing his homework than he does when he is laughing and joking with his parents. But that doesn't mean his underlying personality has changed; all it means is that each situation brings out different aspects of his personality. Neither does it mean that the aspect of personality seen in one particular situation is likely to be seen in another situation.

Even so, situationist psychology serves to remind us that a child's personality can only be fully understood in the light of detailed knowledge of the environment in which he lives. A child may indeed behave in a certain way as a direct result of his surroundings, and the only way to verify this is to look closely at the child in as many different settings as possible. A child who hits his younger sister may, for instance, be regarded as highly aggressive. His parents may assume that aggressiveness is a key component of his personality. Yet, they might find he mixes well with other children, which would suggest that aggressiveness is not one of his essential characteristics but rather a quality that only emerges in interactions with his sister. Indeed, his belligerent attitude towards his sister could well be a reflection of jealousy, not aggression.

Just like me – the effects of modelling

It is undeniable that there are often similarities in behaviour, mannerism and attitudes between parent and child. We all see aspects of our own personality in our children. That could mean that some aspects of personality are inherited. But psychologists offer 'modelling theory' as a more plausible explanation. This theory proposes that, as a child becomes closely attached to his parents and develops a strong positive relationship with them, he begins to take on some of their personal characteristics. This increases the child's self-confidence. Through modelling (or identification) he gradually absorbs the attitudes and behaviour of his mother and father, selecting the characteristics which he finds most desirable. In this way, the child's personality is greatly influenced by the personalities of his parents, especially in the early years. Similarities between parents and child emerge in this way. So the fact that your child's personality is 'just like his father's' has more to do with modelling than with an inherited likeness.

A guide for parents

Your child is not the way he is because 'he was born that way'. Neither is he the way he is because 'you have made him that way'. It is the combination of inherited and environmental characteristics that determine his eventual outcome. These dual influences operate throughout the whole of the child's life. The biggest influence of all is the child's upbringing. The way you respond to your child, the way you love him, guide him, advise him, support him and stimulate him during his childhood lays the foundations for his later life. This book looks at parent–child relationships in detail and examines their impact on child development.

Chapter 3

Is My Child's Behaviour Normal, or is She Disturbed?

All parents worry about their child's behaviour no matter what age the child is. The mother and father of a newborn often worry about its feeding and sleeping habits. Parents of a two-year-old toddler might worry because she seems to have such fierce tantrums. And a four-year-old may cause concern because she is so shy compared to other children of her age. The list of potential worries is endless. Underlying all these worries is the parents' fear that their child's behaviour is not normal. No parent likes to think their child behaves abnormally, but there is no clear line between normality and abnormality.

Defining normality

Some aspects of normality are easier to define than others. Careful study of child development means that professionals now know the physical, intellectual, social and linguistic skills expected of children at each age. These scales are used by psychologists to assess individual child development. (The final section of this book presents this detailed information in clearly marked stages, from birth to five years, and discusses how you can use this information in relation to your own child.) There is no disagreement, for example, that it is normal for a child to be walking by twenty months, that it is normal for a two-year-old child to have a vocabulary of single words, and that it is normal for a four-year-old child to be able to complete a simple jigsaw. But when it comes to defining normal behaviour and emotions, the situation is less clear.

As a parent, you expect certain standards of behaviour from your child – standards which you consider to be normal. In your house, bedtime for a five-year-old might be 7 p.m., the child might be required to tidy away her own toys, and it might be normal for her to have friends to the house after school, whereas in your next-door neighbour's house, bedtime for a five-year-old might be 9 p.m., toys might be cleared away by the parents, and the child might not be allowed to have any friends to her house to play; two standards of 'normality' side by side yet quite different from each other.

This variation in family normality is seen when children interact outside the home. Some parents emphasize the importance of education to their child and encourage her to attend school regularly, to be well-behaved, to try hard at all assignments and to act respectfully towards the class teacher. It would be abnormal for a child from that background to be disinterested in school, to be cheeky to her teacher and to misbehave in class. That type of behaviour would suggest the child has an emotional difficulty which is affecting her behaviour in school. Other parents have a less positive attitude to school. They are resentful of teachers, see little point in education because of the high unemployment rate, and take no interest in their child's schooling. It would not be abnormal for a child from that background to be disinterested in school, to be cheeky to her teacher and to misbehave in class.

Adults tend to form views on normality on the basis of memories from their own childhood. Parents who have had a satisfactory upbringing will often take that as a yardstick when raising a child themselves. And parents who have had an unhappy family life as children will often use that as a yardstick for how their child should not be brought up. Patterns of family life – each with its own idea of normality – tend to be passed down from generation to generation in this way.

The first step in understanding your own view on normality is to identify what you regard as the main goals of childhood.

The goal for your child might be to be happy, or to achieve her maximum potential, or to be a success in school, or to be popular, or to have a strong self-image. The list of potential goals is endless. The next step is to identify the ways in which you think these goals can be achieved. It is permissible for your child to achieve happiness at the expense of others? If so, it will be normal for her to ignore the wishes of her brothers and sisters in order to get what she wants. Is your child allowed to become popular by letting other children play with her toys? If so, then it will be normal for her to lend her toys. Has success in school to be achieved at all costs? If so, then it will be normal for your child to do hours of homework every night. And so it goes on. The aspirations you have for your child and the way you encourage her to realize these goals determine the boundaries of 'normality' in your family.

Parents are often forced to reassess their views on normality when they see their child playing with other children. That's when you start to think that perhaps you are too strict with her (because the other children are allowed more freedom), or that you fuss over her too much (because the other children are allowed to play rough-and-tumble games), or that you don't demand enough of her (because the other children are able to do a lot by themselves), and so on. Of course, you should have an open mind on what you regard as normal. Parents are not infallible and there is always room for change. But don't alter your standards too easily. If you feel your family structure should be modified in some way, consider it seriously before making changes. Certainly discuss your ideas with your partner. Disagreements between parents about the way children should be raised only serve to confuse a child.

Incidence of psychological difficulties in childhood

Calculating the incidence of psychological disturbances in children is problematical due to the wide variety of opinions about what constitutes normality and abnormality. Those studies that have used acceptable criteria for making such judgements about children confirm that most children have emotional or behavioural difficulties at some stage in their development. Fortunately, the difficulties are often temporary. Surveys estimate that only 5–15 per cent of children experience psychological difficulties severe enough to interfere with their development, and only a few of these children need professional help. A great number can be helped by timely and sensible intervention from their parents. (The remaining chapters of this book look at common problem areas in childhood and the ways parents can help their children.)

Why things go wrong

Children can become difficult to manage and parent–child relationships can become strained for many different reasons. Psychological explanations of troubled children depend on the particular perspective of child development that is adopted. The psychoanalytic explanation of a child's disturbed behaviour is in terms of unconscious feelings which break through into consciousness and cause the child to behave uncharacteristically. This explanation requires parents to focus on their child's deeper feelings in an effort to understand what is troubling her. The behaviouristic explanation of a child's disturbed behaviour is in terms of the child's learning to act in that manner. This explanation requires parents to examine the ways they reinforce their child's behaviour, either deliberately or unknowingly. The situationist explanation of a child's disturbed behaviour is in terms of the child's reacting to the specific situation she is in at the time she is misbehaving. This explanation requires parents to pay close attention to the exact circumstances in which their child's disturbed behaviour occurs.

Yet some instances of disruptive or disturbed child behaviour are due to the child's underlying anxiety, some instances are due to parents who inadvertently encourage their child to misbehave, and some instances are direct responses to something specific in the child's situation – though most instances are due to a combination of all these influences. In every instance close attention must be paid to family environment.

Children go through phases

Children go through phases or stages in their development. Sometimes these phases are hard to live with. The 'terrible-twos', for example, is a time associated with tantrums and attention-seeking behaviour, but most children become anti-social and demanding around that age, and so even though the behaviour is worrying it is still within the boundaries of normality. The fact that the behaviour is typical for two-year-olds doesn't make the child any easier to live with, but at least parents should be reassured that tantrums at the toddler stage don't mean the child will be badly behaved for the rest of her life.

Likewise, many three- and four-year-olds go through a phase of independence where they want to do everything themselves. Children of that age often insist on dressing themselves, even though they may not be competent enough to complete the task – and an outburst of temper due to frustration may follow. Although that behaviour is irritating it is a part of normal development. There are many similar phases of childhood where behaviour causes concern even though it follows a pattern seen in nearly every child. These phases usually pass without outside interference.

Individual differences in rates of development

Most children go through the same stages of development at approximately the same age, but there is no such thing as 'the average child'. There are wide individual differences in rates of progress. Also no child makes progress uniformly in all areas of development. A five-year-old might be able to do a lot for herself, as would be expected from a child that age, and yet at the same time have the selfishness of a younger child.

Disturbance and normality have common features

A child's behaviour in itself may not tell you whether your child is disturbed or not. For instance, bed-wetting is the most frequent early-warning sign that a child is under emotional stress, but there are many children who wet the bed simply because they have not been properly trained to be dry at night. Bed-wetting for these children has nothing to do with emotional pressure; it is a normal response to their lack of adequate toilet-training.

In fact, most signs of disturbed behaviour – including jealousy, poor sleeping patterns, aggressiveness, attention-seeking, shyness, tearfulness, boisterousness, withdrawal, anger, irregular eating habits – are found in normal children at some time in their lives. If you are concerned that your child's behaviour might be abnormal you need to examine her actions in the broader context of what is happening in the rest of her life.

Temporary disturbances

Temporary difficulties in children are often eased through timely intervention by parents. Only a small percentage of childhood difficulties progress to a more serious stage. Let's look at the following example:

The problem: Four-year-old Diane had great difficulty settling down at nursery. Every day, without fail, she would become extremely distressed when her mother left her there. While many children are like this in the first few days, most get over this temporary upset quickly. Diane did not.

The observation: Scrutiny of Diane and her mother entering the nursery school revealed a regular pattern to their interaction. As they approached the nursery the child seemed content, but when they reached the door, Diane started to frown. Her mother was very tense, bracing herself for the expected outburst from her child. Crossing the threshold of the nursery, Diane started to cry. The more she became distressed the more her mother became distressed. She spent several minutes trying to calm her down. That did not work. Then she began to shout at her, berating her for behaving like a baby. Her rebukes had no effect either. Ten minutes after entering the nursery Diane's mother finally left her there, giving her one last reassuring hug. Diane waved to her mother as she disappeared from her sight, and at that point one of the nursery staff led Diane gently to play with the other children.

The analysis: Do you think that Diane's behaviour is normal or disturbed? How much is her distressed behaviour a reflection of her fear of leaving her mother and how much is it a reflection of the way her mother is handling the separation? Do you think her mother could do anything to help her daughter, or should she wait to see if she grows out of it? Certainly, it is clear that the mother is as unhappy about leaving her at nursery as Diane is at being left. The mother could take a more positive approach by trying to be calm herself. When she grows anxious as she approaches the nursery, Diane senses this and she too grows anxious. She could give the appearance of calm confidence – even though her stomach is churning with anxiety – and could continually reassure her daughter that everything will be fine. Second, she could shorten the actual moment of separation. Instead of remaining with Diane in the nursery for ten minutes, the mother might come in with her, help her put on her overall, then leave immediately no matter how much the child begs her to stay. Third, Diane's mother could praise her for doing so well when she collects her at the end of each nursery session. These basic measures would go a long way to help the child through her temporary – but normal – upset. Without that sort of sensible and timely intervention from her parents, Diane's disturbance could intensify.

The solution to this temporary disturbance is ostensibly simple, but it requires two actions from Diane's mother. First, she has to recognize that she has a problem, and second, she has to be prepared to modify her own behaviour in order to help her daughter. As a parent, solutions to your child's temporary difficulties are just as likely to involve you as they are to involve your child, and in this way many childhood problems can be overcome before they become serious.

Understanding normality

Despite all these different aspects of normality and abnormality that should be considered when assessing a child's behaviour, there are certain guidelines for judging whether behaviour is psychologically normal or not. While the application of these guidelines will not give you hard-and-fast answers, they will provide you with some ideas to explore further. If you are concerned about certain aspects of your child's emotional state, ask yourself the following questions.

Is my child's behaviour age-appropriate? Is your child's behaviour normally seen in a child of that age or does it usually occur in younger children? Although children vary from each other, the differences should not be extreme. There is no need for parents to worry when their eighteen-month-old infant throws her food about during mealtimes, whereas there is need to worry when a ten-year-old child starts to throw her food around at mealtimes. Behaviour should be age-appropriate.

How long has my child been behaving this way? Many emotional difficulties are transient and are an expected part of normal development. But if the difficulty persists over a long period then there may be something more serious underlying it. For instance, many young children go through phases of not wanting to go to school – perhaps because there is a particular lesson they want to avoid. That is not unusual. However, it would be unusual for a young child to behave this way for more than a few weeks. Time is an important factor in judging the gravity of a child's behaviour.

Has she ever behaved this way before? You can use knowledge of your child's previous behaviour to decide how significant her actions are. If parents know, for example, that their young daughter starts to twiddle her hair whenever she is tired – and that she has had this habit since she was a toddler – they would not regard that as worrying. Yet they would be worried if they had never seen her do that before and she suddenly started the habit at the age of nine or ten. Their awareness that she has had this habit for a long time and their knowledge that it is not linked to anything in particular except tiredness eliminates any worry they might have.

Is the difficulty linked to a specific event? All children are vulnerable when they are under psychological pressure. Some life events are too demanding for young children to cope with – just as some life events are too demanding for some adults to cope with. It is not unusual for a four-year-old to become unsettled, irritable and attention-seeking when her parents are going through the process of a bitter divorce. Few children would behave any differently. Emotional and behavioural difficulties are a normal and understandable childhood reaction to stress. While these disturbed responses still need very sensitive management by parents, they can be resolved.

How severe is the behaviour, and how often does it occur? If you are concerned about something your child is doing, try to determine how often it happens and what exactly occurs. You may well find that the problem is not nearly as worrying as you first thought. Thumb-sucking is fairly common among children. It is only a possible sign of disturbance if the child sucks her thumb continuously, day and night, and becomes upset when told to stop.

Are there other signs of disturbance? A child under stress often displays more than one sign of disturbance. The child who comes home from nursery tearful one day is probably crying because of a particular incident. Perhaps her best friend wouldn't play with her during free-play time. The tears by themselves aren't serious. But the child who is tearful, and at the same time loses her appetite, can't sleep at nights and

Is My Child's Behaviour Normal, or is She Disturbed?

develops a stammer, is unlikely to be responding to something as simple as a one-off incident.

What is the child's perspective of her behaviour? The child may not see anything wrong with the way she is behaving. Hitting her younger brother in order to retrieve her toy might seem perfectly reasonable from her point of view and she might not understand why you are reacting against her. Ask the child why she does it and what she thinks her victim feels like. By having a clearer picture of the child's perspective, you may be better placed to help her change.

How much is the child's behaviour impairing her overall development? An indication of the severity of a child's behaviour is the extent to which it interferes with other aspects of her life. A child may have a fear of dogs and as a result may become agitated when a dog comes close to her. That is normal; but the boundary of abnormality is crossed when the fear is so extreme that the child cries when she sees a picture of a dog, or when dogs are mentioned in conversation, or when she will not leave the house for fear of meeting a dog. At that point, the behaviour is badly affecting her life and as such it is abnormal.

Has she changed suddenly? You have to judge a child's present behaviour in the light of her past behaviour. Bear in mind that what is normal for your child may not be normal for your friend's child, or vice versa. The change in the pattern of behaviour is what matters, especially if that change is sudden and apparently spontaneous. Some children are shy by nature and do not enjoy social events. There is nothing abnormal about this. Yet the outgoing vivacious child who suddenly loses confidence and becomes shy is a cause for concern. That is not to say that established patterns of behaviour are unimportant, just that unexpected changes in a youngster's development are worth your attention.

How have you tried to help your child? Ask parents what they have done to change their child's behaviour. Nine times out of ten they will say, 'We've tried everything, absolutely everything.' Closer investigation usually reveals that they are true to their word, that they have indeed tried everything. Often, though, they have not tried any one method long enough or consistently enough for it to have worked. When you decide on a course of action to change your child's behaviour, stick to it for at least three or four weeks before altering your strategy. Every child needs consistency in her environment.

Worries about normality

There is more to understanding children than simply asking yourself these very basic questions. However, if you are concerned about your child's development these questions will point you in the right direction. In most cases you will realize that what you thought was the end of the world for your child is in fact a passing phase that needs just a little bit of help. Should your worries persist, don't be afraid to seek professional help. A child psychologist would much rather see parents and reassure them that nothing is wrong than have them sitting at home worrying unnecessarily. Referrals to a child psychologist can be made through your health visitor or family doctor. And remember that if the psychologist does feel your child's behaviour is serious then you will be given help.

Chapter 4

Attention

Children need attention no matter what age they are. That is a normal part of child development. Human beings are by nature social animals; we live in social units and we thrive on social relationships with other people. Of course, there are people who are 'loners', people who seem to get on well without being close to anyone. But most individuals want to relate to others in society, and the only way to relate to others is by getting their attention.

Right from birth, the new baby relies totally on adults to meet its needs. Without adult attention, it cannot satisfy hunger or thirst, it cannot keep warm during cold nights, and it cannot even keep clean. The newborn human baby would die without caring adult attention. This basic need becomes evident as soon as the baby enters the world, and continues throughout childhood.

Feeding

The method of feeding the baby does not make much difference to its demands for attention. Leaving aside health considerations (a breast-fed baby has less chance of infection in the early months of life than has a bottle-fed baby), bottle-feeding has the obvious advantage that it does not tie the mother to her baby every few hours. The father can take over for as many feeds as the couple want. That way, by varying the adults who do the feeding, the baby's need for attention is not directed solely to one person. Contrast this with the breast-feeding mother who is by necessity tied to the baby. Only she can meet its demands for the satisfaction of hunger. This means she has to give the baby regular attention day and night, whether she feels like it or not. One way round this is to use a breast pump – which can be hired from the National Childbirth Trust or from La Leche League – for expressing milk so that the mother can have an evening off. But some women find these devices unsuitable and are unable to generate enough breast milk to satisfy the baby in a bottle feed. Choice over the method of feeding is a personal one.

Bonding

A child's need for attention is not only a matter of obtaining physical care. It ensures important emotional care as well. The crying baby will receive comfort from its parents, providing the necessary warmth and security. The smiling infant has fun with his parents, who are quick to respond to his playful antics. These attention-getting devices help develop an emotional relationship between the child and his parents – and it is this relationship that has the greatest influence on his subsequent psychological development. The quality of that affectionate bond determines many of the child's emotional characteristics in later life.

Forming an emotional attachment between mother and child rarely takes place instantly. Some parents do say that they felt 'love at first sight' as soon as they set eyes on their child for the first time. Plenty of parents, however, have mixed emotions when they see their newborn for the first time. Thoughts such as 'Is he healthy?', 'Will we be able to cope?', 'Why doesn't he take his feed properly like the other babies?' and 'Will these forceps marks on his face go away as the doctor says or is he just saying that to calm us down?' are common. These feelings are understandable. Very soon, though, mother and baby begin to mesh together as they get to know each other.

Don't worry if this meshing process takes time. Some

parents fear there is a very short, critical period during which bonding has to take place, and that if it does not happen then it will never happen at all. This idea is based on the process of 'imprinting' found in the animal world. With imprinting, young animals become emotionally attached to any caring adult figure (even to humans in some cases) only during a specific short period at the start of life. If they miss out at that time, they never relate to adult animals later in life. However, there is no evidence at all that humans have a similar critical period. In fact, psychological research has clearly established that emotional connections between parents and their child do not have to be formed during a fixed time span.

Psychologists once thought that breast-feeding forged a closer bond between mother and baby than bottle-feeding did. We now know that is nonsense and that the specific method of feeding in itself has little to do with bonding. What matters is the emotional interaction between the mother and her baby, and that interaction can take place through a bottle or a breast. Anyway, there are many women who don't have the luxury of choosing feeding methods – after the birth, their breasts may not produce enough milk or they may be too unwell to have the energy needed for breast-feeding. And there are some women who simply do not feel comfortable breast-feeding the baby. What matters is the caring way she holds her infant when feeding and the soothing words she speaks. These factors are more important to bonding than whether the milk comes out of a real nipple or a latex nipple. The mother who is not relaxed when breast-feeding, or who is concerned and anxious that breast-feeding is not satisfying her newborn, should not think she is putting the baby at risk psychologically by changing to bottle-feeding.

The process of bonding is gradual. Indeed, the child has to be able to differentiate his mother from every other adult before a unique connection can develop between them. And the baby does not acquire that skill till at least the age of seven months. It is not until then that a reciprocal mother–infant attachment forms; it can take longer. However, children who have not forged secure relationships with at least one adult before their fourth year of life frequently find future personal relationships difficult. In extreme cases, failure to form an emotional connection can lead to an emotional disturbance. Attention from adults, therefore, is necessary for satisfactory development.

Specific features of the mother–child relationship help bonding to occur. But it is not simply a matter of the mother's meeting the baby's physical needs. Neither does it depend on how much time they spend together since bonding does not necessarily happen with the adult who spends most time with the child. This is verified by studies of kibbutz children. In these communal establishments, each baby lives with his family at night while during the day he is looked after by a nurse in the nursery, along with all the other kibbutz children. The baby consequently spends most of his waking hours in the care of an adult other than his mother or father. And yet research confirms in that situation that emotional attachments are still formed more often with the mother than with the nurse.

Important factors that foster the growth of emotional connections between mother and baby include:

- the mother's ability to soothe her child when he is unhappy. Bonds appear strongest in families where the mother feels able to calm her baby down when he is distressed. Her self-confidence plays a part, too; the mother who has a low opinion of her own skills feels incapable of settling her baby, and this in turn increases his distress, which in turn decreases his mother's self-confidence even more. And so a vicious circle – which is hard to break – can arise. Mothers suffering from post-natal depression often say they have had this type of experience, especially in the baby's first year.
- frequent physical contact, of a loving kind, when the baby is fractious and unsettled. Although physical contact by itself does not guarantee the formation of an attachment, the mother who strokes and cuddles her baby when he is upset is more likely to form an emotional connection with him.
- the mother's sensitivity to her baby's signals when he is

demanding her attention. It is not always easy to make sense of a baby's particular behaviour. Crying after breakfast might mean he has a build-up of wind, while the same behaviour later on in the day might mean he is bored and wants a bit of adult attention. Parents gradually get to know their own baby and develop an understanding of what the baby is communicating to them. That sensitivity to the child's signals enhances the emotional attachment between them.

- the degree of control that the infant has over his own environment. Child-care at home can be very routine, very perfunctory, because that is the easiest way of running an orderly home. And there is no doubt that some form of routine helps a child cope with the world around him. A consistent and well-structured environment can give a child a strong feeling of self-confidence and security, but there should be flexibility. Psychologists claim that a child who is not allowed to make any choices in his daily routine – whether it is choosing the clothes he wears, or what biscuits he has at tea-time, or what toys he is allowed to play with – has greater difficulty bonding with his mother than does a child who is involved in making decisions about what he does.

Of course, your child can form attachments with more than one person, not just with you, and so he is as likely to form an emotional attachment with his father as he is with his mother. In today's society where fathers take a much more involved part in their infant's care, the chances of bonding between father and baby are high.

The crying baby

A crying baby needs your attention, even though you may not know precisely why he is crying. Every parent has to deal with that situation at some stage. The first action to be taken when a baby cries constantly is to arrange for a full medical examination. Of course you have to check for the more obvious possibilities, such as whether the baby needs changing, or whether a nappy pin is jabbing into him. Having eliminated these factors, ensure that he is physically fit. That is the first priority. There is an endless list of physical complaints that can underlie a baby's constant distress and your GP has to investigate them.

'Colic' is the term most frequently applied to the baby who cries regularly, especially if the infant is under the age of three months. Colic refers to a pain in the stomach caused by a spasm in the tummy muscles, and is given that name because babies with the condition often pass a great deal of wind. While colic is a convenient explanation of a baby's distress, it is extremely difficult to verify. In fact, the diagnosis of colic can become self-confirming because the constantly crying baby – irrespective of why he is upset – will virtually always release enormous belches of air every so often. When that happens the worried parents breathe a sigh of relief in the belief that this excess wind was causing his upset. Yet the very act of continuous crying makes a baby suck in vast amounts of air. So it is just as likely that the expulsion of wind is the result of crying, not the cause of it.

Recent research into food additives suggests a link between certain chemical additives, used in many commercially prepared foods, and behavioural disturbances in babies and young children. The first to promote this idea was an American medical practitioner, B. Feingold. He claimed that if a disruptive child only takes natural products, without any chemical additives and without the chemical 'salicylate' (which occurs naturally in tomatoes), then the child's behaviour will improve. The same claims were made about crying babies. But evidence to support these claims is unclear. Just as many research studies show no change in behaviour when a child is put on an additive-free diet as those studies that do report improvement. Even so, it is possible that a crying baby may be allergic to a particular type of milk. There is no harm in changing the milk in order to see if it has an effect on the amount of crying. A mother with a constantly crying baby may be at a loss what to do next. The act of changing her baby's diet returns some control to her. Even if the diet change has no impact on the actual level of the crying, that regained feeling of control may increase the mother's self-confidence – a factor that could help her through the crisis.

Anxiety usually plays a large part in the family with a crying baby, and it can become self-reinforcing. The mother with a crying baby – even when the baby is in the habit of crying as a result of a physical ailment – often develops the automatic expectation that her baby will cry every night. And so she becomes tense and agitated at the prospect of another horrendous night. The baby senses her tension, reacting to it by becoming tense and tearful. So the mother's initial reaction over her anticipation of her baby's crying actually brings out the behaviour she dreads. If you find yourself in that situation, keep calm. Calmness is extremely influential in settling a distressed baby. Whether you use relaxation exercises learned in the antenatal class, or whether you use imagery to achieve a state of calmness, the main objective is to relax – without using artificial methods such as drugs or alcohol.

Failure to form emotional bonds with the mother can result in a distressed baby, a baby who feels alone, a baby who cries all the time. Some babies who cry persistently do so because they simply feel sad and alone. When considering the crying baby, therefore, psychologists always suggest looking at the mother–child relationship to assess whether it is satisfying emotionally for them both, and to ascertain whether the mother feels comfortable with her baby. In some instances – such as post-natal depression, where the mother's own depression directly upsets her baby's psychological development – the cause of the difficulty is obvious. In other instances, the difficulties may be more subtle and can be related to the mother's own upbringing when she was a child. A woman who had a sterile relationship with her mother may find difficulties relating to her own children.

But a poor mother–child relationship is not the only cause of crying in babies. Sometimes attention-seeking behaviour underlies an infant's perpetual screaming, just as it often underlies a child's constant tantrums.

Understanding Children

The attention-seeking child

Babies and young children seem to have the knack of pushing their parents to the absolute limit with their demands to be the star attraction and are able to turn any situation to their own advantage. It is as if they have an intuitive knowledge of their parents' weak spots – like the baby who starts crying once again just as his mother thinks she has lulled him into sleep, or like the toddler who has a screaming tantrum in the supermarket just as his mother reaches the check-out. The attention-seeking child is normal but aggravating.

That does not mean parents are unable to change the way their child behaves. The first step you have to take when trying to counter the demands of the attention-seeking child, whether a three-month-old baby or three-year-old child, is to understand what is happening. And to do that properly you have to understand some elementary principles of learning theory – because there is an element of learning involved in his behaviour.

When a child is born there are certain actions he does automatically by reflex. For example, a baby cries for its very first feed, even though he has no idea that crying will result in food coming to him. An infant will grasp a finger placed in his hand. The toddler who falls over automatically puts his hands out to protect himself from the fall. These acts of behaviour occur instinctively without the child's having to think about them.

Yet most things that children do have to be learned. A baby learns that the sight of a bottle coming towards him means that he is about to be fed. The young child learns to tidy his toys away because his father shows he is pleased, and the child likes this. He also learns not to touch fragile ornaments in the house because that behaviour incurs a reprimand, and he does not like this. Children differ at the rate they learn how to behave, but the underlying principles of learning are always the same:

- *if something that a child regards as positive immediately follows one of his actions, then there is a high probability that he will repeat the*

same action in the future. The link between his behaviour and the favourable result reinforces the child's desire to do it again.
- *if something that a child regards as negative immediately follows one of his actions, then there is a lower probability that he will repeat that same action in the future.* The link between his behaviour and the unfavourable result diminishes the child's desire to do it again.

This seems simple enough. And if that is all there was to bringing up children then parents would have an easy time of it. However, there is another principle of learning in children:

- *a child may like a certain event even though his parents do not.* It is not always easy to appreciate exactly what it is that a child enjoys. Many babies and young children would rather have any form of adult attention in preference to any type of material object. So although the parents may think that a smack on the bottom will discourage their child from misbehaving, that reprimand for a disruptive action actually may be attractive from the pre-schooler's point of view. After all, negative attention is better than no attention at all. There are situations where a parental rebuke can actually encourage the very behaviour that it is intended to eliminate. For example, even though the baby's father might be furious with him for crying at night when everyone else in the house is trying to sleep, the expression of that fury means the baby is getting his father's full attention.

Consistent management

The application of these theoretical principles about the way a child learns behaviour leads to practical suggestions for dealing effectively with the attention-seeking child.

- *give him what he wants – that is, attention – but give it at varying times for different actions.* You have to control when the child is given attention. If you only attend to your child when he is being naughty, then he will quickly learn to be naughty every time he wants attention. So be prepared to give the child attention spontaneously, when he is not expecting it. Play with your baby when he is settled and contented. Praise your child when he is being well-behaved. Give him a cuddle, or a pat on the head, or whatever, when he is watching television quietly. Of course, the child may push you away because at that point he would rather watch what is happening on the screen. Yet your unexpected cuddle can be sufficient to meet the child's emotional needs. It takes away the necessity to misbehave in order to get attention.

- *try to ignore negative attention-seeking behaviour*. There are many occasions when punishment seems to have no effect whatsoever, except perhaps to encourage the child to carry on misbehaving. Ignoring the undesirable behaviour can be very effective. But it is difficult. Requiring your strong resolve, a solid refusal to respond to the child's negative attention-seeking behaviour can discourage it. Parents may be ambivalent when it comes to ignoring a crying baby. No one feels comfortable leaving a baby alone when it is crying, but there can be a place for this in your management of your baby. You have to use your own judgement, however, about the suitability of this strategy. If you do decide to ignore your baby when he cries, make sure you look in on him regularly – without letting him see you, of course.

Both these principles have to be applied consistently if they are to have an impact on the child's behaviour. You will not see much change in your baby's rate of crying if you ignore him for, say, thirty seconds then turn round and scream at him. Similarly, there is no point in making a special effort one day to praise the child because he is behaving well, then letting two weeks lapse before you do the same again. You have to be consistent in what you do.

Consider three-year-old Eric. He is typical of the attention-seeking pre-schooler. He often sits down with his parents and his seven-year-old sister to watch televison at the end of the day. Without fail he tries to draw attention to himself. At first, he rocks his chair about, distracting everyone from listening. Then he begins to hum a tune. His mother tells Eric to be quiet, but he continues. Then his father and sister go through the same routine. They all then decide to ignore him. The tension increases. Eventually, the boy shouts so loud that he drowns the sounds coming from the television set. At that point his parents can take no more. In temper they take Eric upstairs to his own room where he causes further disruption by screaming as loud as he can. Another family moment has been spoiled by the child's attention-seeking behaviour.

Suppose you are Eric's parent. How would you handle the situation? If you look closely at what is going on, you will see that at first his parents give him attention – in the form of reprimands, but attention all the same – then they change their minds and try to ignore him. Eventually they give him their full attention again when his noises become too distracting. This inconsistency in their approach does nothing to discourage the child from behaving this way. As well as that, Eric gets attention only when he misbehaves. Perhaps if he was sitting on his father's knee getting a cuddle while watching television, this might satisfy his need for attention. Consistent and well-planned management is needed.

A background of love

Do not lose sight of the fact that you and your child are in a loving relationship. It is very easy to become mechanistic when trying to manage a child who is constantly demanding attention. Parents can hide behind a system of rules quite easily because rules mean you do not have to think about what you are doing. But a parent–child relationship without love is a sterile relationship. A parent–child relationship that is inflexible is a sterile relationship. And a parent-child relationship that is more concerned with controlling the child than developing his potential is a sterile relationship. Applying rules does not mean emotions have to take second place. So when you do decide to be consistent with your child, do not take it to extremes. Couple the application of rules with sensitivity to your child's emotional needs.

Children fluctuate in their demands for attention. For instance, the two-year-old infant is at the stage when he wants to be independent. One way to show that independence is to make his parents do what he wants, and so he may seek attention at that age because he wants to be in charge.

Sometimes a child seeks attention because he is insecure. A child who starts nursery school might feel vulnerable and afraid. The challenge of leaving the warmth of the parental home for the care of strangers can be very daunting. In that situation a child frequently demands attention, not as a result of the way his parents are handling him, but because he lacks confidence to tackle the demands of being at nursery. Likewise, a child who is feeling unwell will seek attention. Parental attention for the sick child is often more therapeutic than any medicinal treatment. All these reactions are normal. So rules in themselves are not the panacea for coping with the attention-seeking child. You have to look to the child's individual circumstances as well.

As with babies, there are some children whose demand for attention is so extreme that it indicates there is an underlying emotional problem. This often occurs when there is a breakdown in the parent–child relationship. The child becomes attention-seeking as a result of his insecurity and unhappiness. In such instances, professional involvement may be necessary to help the child through his difficulty, but before reaching that conclusion, be sure you have made sufficient efforts to apply the above principles consistently, and be sure there is nothing in particular that could be troubling him.

Chapter 5

Comforters

A comforter is any object that makes a child feel happier, more confident and more secure, when she is tired or distressed. Most children have an attachment to some such object – an item that brings them more tranquillity than anything else can. One child might like to hold a teddy she has had for years, even though it is ragged with its eyes and ears pulled off long ago, while another child might prefer her cot blanket, even though it is well worn. You may be amazed at the value the child places on such a scruffy object. The smell of the comforter, the way it looks, and the way it feels, are what matter to the child.

Why comforters

Psychologists consider that the use of comforters originates from the very early sucking response of the newborn baby. In the early weeks of life the baby finds that sucking is an enjoyable activity in more ways than one. After all, not only does it bring the satisfaction of hunger, it also becomes associated with loving care. The method of feeding in itself really doesn't matter. If the mother is breast-feeding, then sucking gives the baby oral contact with her. If the mother is bottle-feeding then sucking still gives the baby close physical contact with her. Through either feeding method, the baby learns to regard the repetitive sucking motions as being very pleasant. Most babies start to suck even when they are not feeding. This non-nutritive sucking can be seen in babies a few weeks old, especially as they drift off to sleep in the pram. Already the psychological foundations for comforters are established.

The comforter becomes a way of reliving an earlier life-experience that brought emotional satisfaction. Although the maturing child learns to obtain satisfaction in other ways, that does not eradicate the pleasant recall of babyhood. A comforter gives a child a sense of security because she associates warmth and kindness with it. Even though this association is forged early on in the child's life, it remains strong in the later years.

Comfort habits

A child may obtain a similar feeling of security and tranquillity from a comfort habit, rather than from a particular object. Thumb-sucking is the most common example. Most parents associate this with immaturity and discourage their child from persisting with the habit. However, thumb-sucking in a young child is not harmful, though in an older child it might indicate a strong sense of emotional insecurity.

There are dental considerations as well. Continuation of the habit beyond the age of five may cause damage to the child's second set of teeth, by pushing them out of shape, if the habit continues long enough. When that happens, corrective dental treatment is necessary.

If you do want to help your child stop thumb-sucking, then:

DO

- *aim to decrease the habit gradually, in stages.* Just as an adult who wants to give up smoking often finds it easier to do so gradually, so too does a child who has to stop thumb-sucking. Set a time scale of, say, eight weeks, during which time you hope to eliminate the habit.
- *tell the child what you are trying to achieve.* Let her know that you want her to stop thumb-sucking and that you are going to help her. Each time you move from one phase to the next explain what you are trying to achieve.

Comforters

- *explain to your child why she should stop.* Use terms the child can understand: for instance, that other children think she is babyish, or her best friend doesn't suck his thumb, or her teeth will be damaged, and so on. A child of three and upwards will understand what you are saying.
- *be prepared to give your child lots of encouragement, especially the first time she has to go without sucking her thumb.* She may be feeling miserable at the prospect of having to do without her comfort habit.
- *select one short occasion, during which your child usually sucks her thumb, and use that as your starting point.* It might be when she is watching television, or perhaps when you are reading a story to her. Give the child advance warning that you don't want her to suck her thumb on that specific occasion on that specific day.
- *tell the child what her reward will be when the target is met.* For example, an extra five minutes' playing before she goes to bed can be an effective incentive.
- *slowly increase the number of occasions the child has to do without thumb-sucking.* Build up gradually from, say, once every two days, to once every day, to twice every day, and so on. Decide on a clear plan of action and stick to it. The habit could take several weeks to eliminate.
- *give lots of praise when you see progress is being made.* Each day that you see the thumb-sucking decreasing in frequency, let your child know that you are pleased. Make a big fuss of her achievements.
- *make sure your child does not have an underlying worry that could be making her feel insecure.* Take a close look at your child's life, since there may be some factor which is causing her stress. If there is, attend to that rather than just to the thumb-sucking itself.

DON'T

- *expect the habit to stop overnight.* The child will take time to stop, because it gives her pleasure.
- *use techniques based on avoidance principles.* Strategies, such as

painting the child's finger with a nasty-tasting solution, or covering the offending thumb in sticking-plaster, rarely work. In most cases, that approach only intensifies the child's resistance to giving up. Of course, you may get lucky and see the habit vanish instantly, but if you take an aversive approach you run the risk of confrontation.
- *make a mountain out of a molehill.* Start pressurizing the child too much about her thumb-sucking and you may make her so anxious that it actually increases.
- *forget that gentle coaxing to stop a comfort habit is more effective than a dogmatic approach.* Forcing a child to stop only ends in a battle. Keep things in perspective.

Masturbation is another comfort habit that embarrasses parents. Yet masturbation is not at all harmful. Manipulation of the genitals to bring pleasure and relaxation is a phenomenon found in every society. Nearly all boys or girls explore their genitals at some stage, just as they explore their noses, ears, and other body parts. Most parents find the habit embarrassing because they associate it with adult masturbation which culminates in orgasm. But child masturbation gives comfort, not sexual stimulation. The guidelines suggested above for the elimination of thumb-sucking apply equally to the elimination of masturbation. And don't be tempted to use the old wives' tales. Threats of blindness, or warts, or whatever, will only frighten the child, and she will learn to associate her genitals with fear.

Sucking dummies is probably the only comforting habit that some parents deliberately encourage. A dummy is specially shaped to fit the contours of a young mouth, and is designed so that it cannot be swallowed. Most dummies are made of plastic, are non-toxic, and can be washed and sterilized. Aside from using dummies attached to a bottle in order to feed the baby with milk, parents usually let their child use a dummy on its own for two main reasons. First, to silence the child; placing a dummy in your child's mouth is a sure way of getting her to be quiet, and that is often preferable to having her screaming while you are trying to talk to someone.

Comforters

Second, to help the child fall asleep; a dummy may bring about a state of sleep in a tired infant – something you may be desperate to achieve. In both these instances, a dummy can be a quick and effective way of achieving the desired goal.

If you do let your child use a dummy, make sure it is clean and germ free. Many children take enormous pleasure from throwing their dummy to the ground, and this runs the risk of the child placing a dirty object in her mouth. Sterilize the dummy regularly, otherwise your child may pick up an infection, and that is hardly likely to bring your child peace and tranquillity. Another danger in encouraging a child to use a dummy is that it can create a dependence on an object where it didn't exist before. You may find that your child wants the dummy at other times, apart from when she is tired or unhappy, and that the habit is hard to eliminate once it has started. Yet the judicial use of a dummy can bring about the desired effect. Be prepared to wean the child off it at some point when she is a little older.

There are many other forms of comfort habit which are seen in young children. Nearly all these habits involve rhythmical movement. A child might twist her ear repetitively, twiddle with her hair, rock back and forth in her cot, or even bang her head against the side of the cot. Babies are comforted by that type of repeated rhythmical motion. These comfort habits are harmless in moderation.

Out of control

Excessive use of a comforter can be a sign that a child's lack of security is extreme. If the child cannot go anywhere without a comforter, then her dependence has become too great and this is usually a result of emotional stress. Rather than getting annoyed at the child for behaving in this way, parents have to take a closer look at her life in order to establish why she feels so insecure. There can be many reasons for this, even though some of these might seem trivial to adults. Failing to get something right in school, having a poor relationship with parents, getting into trouble frequently, not being invited to a birthday party, catching a cold, noticing that a pet is unwell, or a family bereavement, can all undermine the well-being of a young child.

The transition from being a normal comfort habit to an indication of something more serious is often gradual. Mary is four years old. Her comforter is a piece of her old cot blanket that she likes to rub against her cheek, and she takes the comforter to bed at night, snuggling into it as she falls asleep. When she was three, her need for the comforter slowly intensified to the point where she was not prepared to go out of the house unless she had her old cot blanket with her. At first her parents made a joke about it and tried to cajole her out of the habit. This seemed to make matters worse. The more they insisted she couldn't take the blanket with her when she went out, the tighter the child held on to it. Tantrums would ensue when she had to leave the comforter behind and she would continue to be tearful until it was back in her clutches.

Mary's parents tried to wean her off the blanket. They offered the child rewards if she would go without the comforter for even one or two occasions, and reminded her that other children of her age did not behave that way. They did not lose their tempers, nor did they try to bully her into acquiescence. But none of their tactics had any effect. Mary still clung to her blanket as though it were a life-line. Realizing the child's need for the blanket had gone beyond being the normal habit it once was, her parents decided to delve further.

Their starting point was the nursery which Mary attended daily. She had been there for several months and appeared to have settled in well. When her mother spoke to the nursery staff about her increased use of the comforter they mentioned that Mary had recently fallen out with her best friend in the nursery. The result was that Mary was lonely.

Her parents recognized that this was the likely reason for her feeling of insecurity. The temporary strain of breaking the friendship had forced the child to return to her comforter for security. The greater her distress became as time went on, the stronger became her need for the comforter. If you were Mary's parents, what would you have done in that situation? How would you have helped the child through this upsetting phase of her life?

Mary's parents decided the best approach would be to boost her confidence instead of focusing on removal of the comforter itself. They made particular efforts to invite some of the nursery children to the house over the next few weeks so that Mary would have a chance to make new friends. That proved to be a successful strategy and helped restore her self-confidence. She did not seem to need the comforter as much. Her parents were delighted to find that gentle discouragement from holding the blanket wherever she went was all that was needed to wean her off it. By looking beyond the physical use of the comforter into the wider background of their child, Mary's parents had been able to identify the source of the child's anxiety, and take appropriate action to help her regain her feeling of security.

Positive use of comforters

Comforters can be used positively to help a child through a difficult experience. There are many situations where the calculated introduction of a comforter to the child can boost her self-confidence enough to cope with stress. These include:

- *hospitalization:* a great many children end up in hospital as a result of an accident or ill-health. Being allowed to take a favourite toy into the hospital ward will make the child feel more at ease, and she will be vulnerable without it. There is no harm in letting her have her comforter for this one-off event.
- *holidays:* strange rooms with unfamiliar noises can make a child distressed when she is trying to sleep at nights. Having her favourite blanket drawn over her bed can ease the child's anxious feelings. It will make the child's holiday more enjoyable as well as your own.

Chapter 6

Aggression

Parents often convey conflicting attitudes to aggression in their children. Aggression in some circumstances is acceptable (when the child has to protect himself, or when he is trying to win a sporting race), but in other circumstances aggression is unacceptable (for example, when a child hits another in order to gain control of a toy). The ability to judge when aggression is socially acceptable develops gradually throughout a child's life, and depends on the experiences he has, and on the attitude of his parents. Children need guidance on the control of their aggression. But where does aggression come from, what causes it, what regulates it, and what influences the development of aggression in your children?

Innate aggression

Freud believed that a baby is born with a measure of aggression, and that parenthood involves teaching the child to repress these hostile impulses. Yet no matter how well parents do their job, according to Freud, these aggressive impulses are always there in the child, just lying under the surface waiting to be triggered off. He regarded child development as a constant battle between the child's instinctively aggressive desires – known as the 'id' – and the outside world: not a very pleasant view of the young child. However, the explanation of innate aggression can account for many of the aggressive actions that mar human society.

But it cannot be as simple as that; we all know at least one child who is very docile, who would never fight back even to save himself from injury. Children like that seem to lack all aggressive urges, even when they themselves are at risk. If human aggression were solely a matter of instinct then such children would not exist.

Social influences

Societies vary in their attitudes to the expression of aggression, and these influence the people living in those societies. The Great Whale River Eskimos, living in the northern reaches of Canada, have a society without any aggression towards children or adults. No act of hostility towards another person is permitted. Children of these Eskimos are not allowed to fight with each other and even aggression at the toddler stage is forbidden. Instead, the children are encouraged to release their aggressive urges on inanimate objects. A lot of Great Whale River snowmen probably get their heads knocked off by angry young children, but surely that is a lot better than the children hurting each other.

The Great Whale River Eskimos believe aggression can be controlled through social influences. Contrast that peace-loving society with the Kwoma tribe of natives from New Guinea. These tribesmen take the opposite view: expression of aggression is positively valued in the Kwoma society. The adults regard it as a useful way of releasing tension. Children are reprimanded and physically punished if they show signs of submissiveness, whereas the child who retaliates aggressively against any attacker receives rewards. Kwoma parents regard themselves as failures if they raise a child who doesn't want to fight.

The influence of television

As parents, you may be concerned that programmes on television are encouraging your child to be aggressive. Viewing figures consistently show that almost 25 per cent of British children under the age of five watch television after nine o'clock in the evening. Many of these programmes show scenes of violence. It is worrying to think that so many young children are watching programmes designed to satisfy the interests of the more mature adult mind. There have been many research studies into this problem, however, and there is not one that shows any link between a child's level of aggression and the number of violent television programmes watched.

One explanation for this lack of connection is 'the dilution factor' – no matter how aggressive or violent one particular television programme might be, its possible influence on the young mind is diluted by the effect of the many non-violent programmes the child also watches. The importance of the dilution factor leads to practical advice for guiding your child's viewing habits.

- *make sure he has a varied diet of television programmes*. Don't let him watch only programmes that are violent action-adventures. Insist that his viewing includes children's entertainment programmes and children's drama programmes as well.
- *do not leave any X-rated videos lying about the home*. Your child could be watching them unsupervised at six in the morning while you are still fast asleep in bed.

Television literacy – the ability to evaluate critically what is shown on television – can be taught to young children. Talking to your child about the violence he watches on the screen will have an effect on his appreciation and understanding of it. Spend some time with the child, explaining to him that television is not real, and that he should not imitate what he sees on television because it is only make believe.

Parental influence

The greatest influence on the expression and development of aggression in young children is the way they are raised by their parents. Numerous studies have investigated the effects of different styles of parenting. The term 'restrictive' describes parents who have very fixed and narrow guidelines for acceptable behaviour, who are adamant in administering punishment every time their child infringes these guidelines, and who discourage their child's tendencies towards independent thought and action. The term 'permissive' describes parents who avoid fixed rules, who do not apply punishment, and who encourage their child to fulfil his own desires irrespective of the feelings of others. You may have met parents who fit neatly into one or other of these categories, although most mothers and fathers adopt a combination of both styles.

Research results confirm that permissive parents have children who are more aggressive than children who have restrictive parents. This is probably because the child raised in a permissive family environment never receives discouragement for aggressiveness and so quickly learns that aggression is a useful way of achieving his goals. That does not mean the answer to aggression is to be restrictive with your child. Children of overly strict parents usually experience intense feelings of frustration, which they are not allowed to release at home. The child in these circumstances is likely to be aggressive as soon as he gets outside the house, frequently when he attends playgroup, nursery or school.

Aggression in young children can be a result of other family influences. Psychological research has shown that where parents use physical punishment to discourage their child's aggressiveness, this may actually increase his aggression. Aggressive parents are likely to have aggressive children. It is always tempting to smack a child when he repeatedly misbehaves, but you can hardly expect your child to behave differently from the way you do. You are the main figures on which your child models his own behaviour. So if you use aggression to get your own way at home, do not be surprised when your child adopts a similar strategy. A child is also more likely to be aggressive when his parents are uncertain about the way he should be managed at home, when his parents have low self-esteem themselves, and when they disagree about how their children should be raised.

All this presents a somewhat confusing picture. But out of all the different research results, a number of clear principles emerge. These guidelines apply to all parents and children:

DO

- *strike a balance in the way you control your child.* This is not always easy to achieve, especially when you are irritable at the end of a long hard day. The most effective style of parenting is one in which a reasonable level of control is exercised over the child.

- *remember that one aim of parenthood is to help your child develop into a well-balanced individual who can cope with the stresses and strains of everyday life.* Parenting is not simply about raising well-controlled obedient children. A warm, caring relationship between child and parent is the most fruitful way of dealing with aggression.

- *sort out your ideas on discipline when your child is out of earshot.* Decide on your methods of punishment and reward between yourselves, well in advance, and then stick to them. Arguing about discipline in front of your child will weaken the effectiveness of your control. The child is likely to become more aggressive in these circumstances.

- *use non-physical methods for punishing your child when he is being aggressive.* There are many other forms of punishment more effective than a smack on the bottom. Most children, for instance, hate being put out of a room for being naughty, or being sent to bed ten minutes early, or being denied their favourite television programme, or being refused their daily ration of sweets. These measures will have more positive impact on your child than will any physical punishment.

- *use verbal methods as well to deal with aggression.* Talk to your child. Even at the age of three or four a child is old enough

Aggression

to understand an explanation that takes the feelings of others into account. You will find that the child can appreciate your arguments against aggression when you couch them in terms of why he should consider the feelings of other people.

- *use explanations that are meaningful to the child.* He may not understand the reasoning 'aggression is bad and so you shouldn't hit people', but he will understand the reasoning 'if you keep on hitting your friends, they won't invite you to their birthday parties'.

- *teach your child socially acceptable ways of releasing aggression.* Painting, clay-modelling and Plasticine are particularly suitable for this purpose. Every day, in playgroups, nurseries, schools and houses, you will find children slapping clay around most vigorously, or perhaps splashing paint enthusiastically on a blank sheet of paper. This is a socially acceptable – and psychologically healthy – way of releasing pent-up emotions. So is any form of physical exercise, like running, football, boxing, skipping, and so on.

DON'T

- *be extreme when dealing with your child.* Extremes of parental behaviour, whether extreme restrictiveness or extreme permissiveness, will always produce aggression in children.

- *use aggression yourself when you see your child being aggressive to others.* Smacking your child when you see him hitting one of his friends does provide a short-term answer – most children are momentarily afraid of physical punishment – but in the long term your aggressive actions will only encourage his aggression.

- *try to bully a child into behaving the way you want him to.* Shouting at a child does have an immediate effect. He will almost certainly stop what he is doing because he is temporarily terrorized by your response. Yet, without full understanding of why he is being chastised, he will probably repeat the behaviour as soon as he is out of your sight.

Understanding Children

- *expect a child under the age of five to see the world the way you do.* Adults know that being on the receiving end of aggression is unpleasant. A young child, however, has to learn that, and teaching him that is part of your job as his parents.

- *confuse aggressive behaviour with aggressive feelings.* Most children will have aggressive emotions from time to time. That is normal. There is nothing wrong if a child feels angry and hostile towards someone, especially when that person has deliberately hurt him. What is wrong is for the child to act on these feelings. The child has to learn how to express his aggressive feelings in an indirect way, without assaulting another person. So do not get angry when you see your child charged with rage – just be sure to help him dissipate that rage without hurting anyone.

Chapter 7

Jealousy

Jealousy is one of the more unpleasant human characteristics; it is a mixture of resentment, fear, insecurity, possessiveness and suspicion – not the sort of emotion we readily admit to. Jealousy is always a very destructive feeling. At best, it causes unhappiness and dissatisfaction to the individual experiencing it, and at worst it results in hurtful actions against other people.

A child can be jealous of other children, whether in her family or not, when she thinks she is being treated less favourably than they. She can be jealous about possessions, either hoarding her own or wanting another child's. A child may be jealous when she sees her parents giving their attention to another child. Such emotions are natural, and the universality of jealousy is reflected throughout children's literature. Some of the best-loved fairy tales have jealousy as their central theme. In *Snow White and the Seven Dwarfs*, the queen constantly asks 'Mirror, mirror, on the wall, Who is the fairest of them all?' Her jealousy for Snow White torments her throughout the whole story. Likewise, Cinderella's rough treatment at the hands of her two ugly sisters stems from their jealousy of her.

An early start

A child starts to feel jealousy for the first time when she realizes that she does not have her mother to herself all the time. At around six months, the child recognizes that there are others in the world and may show jealousy when she sees her mother cuddling another baby. But she learns to cope with this jealousy as she becomes more confident in her relationship with her parents. When the child starts to realize her parents' attention to someone else does not detract from their love for her, then her distress lessens.

The first major incident to arouse a child's jealous emotions is the arrival of a new baby in the family. Until that moment, the first-born child has had her parents all to herself and has not had to compete with anyone in order to be the centre of attention. She expects this way of life to continue for ever. Small wonder that the impending birth of a new brother or sister makes her feel threatened, insecure and jealous. Until she adapts to the new family structure, her feelings of jealousy may dominate. (Ways of preparing your first-born child for the birth of another child in the family are discussed in detail in Chapter 9.)

The age-gap between the children is an important influence on the strength of the first-born child's jealousy. There is no ideal age-gap since much depends on the individual child and the parents. In the same way as a large age-gap between the children can cause jealousy because the older child is well used to being on her own with her parents, a small age-gap can also produce jealousy because the children are likely to have similar desires and interests and are more likely to compete with each other.

Parents usually find that an age difference of about sixteen to eighteen months or less between the first-born child and the baby results in no jealousy. The older child seems less vulnerable at that age. When the age-gap increases to between two and four years, jealousy is much more likely, and then it becomes much less likely once again when the gap is five years and beyond. Yet family planning should take into account factors other than the first-born child's possible jealousy. A small age-gap between children has financial advantages. The unit-cost of each child decreases because clothes can be passed from child to child, as can baby-care equipment, such as bottle sterilization kits, cots, changing mats, and so on. On the other hand, parents might feel they are not ready to cope with another baby until their first-born child is older and more independent. In any case, conception doesn't always occur at the most convenient times. The best laid plans . . .

Sibling rivalry

Jealousy between children in a family – sibling rivalry – is a normal state of affairs, which arises because children have to share their parents' attention, their time, their interests and their financial resources. Many family arguments are caused by jealousy between the children. Sometimes this rivalry continues well into adulthood. The oldest child is most prone to jealousy because she is the only one used to undivided attention from her parents. But even the youngest child will have moments when she is convinced everyone else in the family gets more than she does.

Every child needs individual attention from her parents, no matter her age or developmental stage. Some children are less obvious in demonstrating this need, but it exists all the same. Simple logistics dictate that the more children there are in a family then the less time there is to go round. But whatever time there is, some of it should be spent with each child on her own, whether it is reading a story to her at bedtime, taking her for a walk in the park, or whatever.

Children are often convinced that they themselves are getting a 'raw deal' while their brothers and sisters are somehow more favourably treated. This can be most infuriating because your child may identify an area of discrimination that she thinks exists even though you see no such inequality. The perennial cry of the young child, 'That's not fair', indicates her feelings of injustice and jealousy, even though you may know there is no justification for the accusation. Don't dismiss these statements out of hand. If the child feels strongly enough to voice her opinion of unfair treatment, then she deserves to be heard. Ask her why she feels that way. Her answer will probably be based on a series of statements concerning how much her brother or sister is allowed to do compared to her, or how little pocket money she gets compared to them, without taking account of any age difference that exists between them. You have to explain, for instance, that her brother stays up later at night because he is older and does not require as much sleep; or that her younger sister doesn't have to wash the dishes after meals because she is too young to handle the crockery carefully. Sensible explanations are more likely to appeal to the child's sense of reason than shouted exhortations like 'You go to bed when I decide, whether your brother is in bed or not.'

There will be times when one of your children is allowed to do something forbidden to your other child, simply because they have different skills. Your older child may be permitted to draw with felt-tip pens because she uses them very carefully without making a mess, while a younger child might be allowed to use only coloured pencils because she usually ends up getting ink all over her clothes. That will seem unfair to the child who is denied something available to her brother or sister and, again, you have to explain to the child why you are discriminating in this way.

You may be tempted to encourage one of your children either to behave better or to try harder at school, by comparing her to one of her brothers or sisters. But this technique is unlikely to have the desired effect. Instead, it is virtually guaranteed to intensify sibling rivalry. Judging a younger child's achievements in comparison to those of her older brother or sister will only make her feel inadequate. And the older child may not like such a comparison either. Each child should be accepted as an individual or else feelings of jealousy will emerge. A more effective measure to encourage a child to behave in certain ways is to use her brother's or sister's superior skills as a 'carrot', rather than as a 'stick'. The younger child who is struggling to learn to read will benefit more from her older brother's help with her reading homework than she will from an unfavourable comparison. Such actions are likely to enhance relationships between children, instead of promoting jealousy.

Jealousy

A child with brothers and sisters may be afraid that she is loved less than the others in the family, and may interpret all your behaviour as confirmation of that. Adequate emotional development depends on the child feeling that she is loved as much as the others in the family, no matter what her individual strengths and weaknesses are. Some parents do find that they care for one child in particular, for many different reasons. Perhaps it is because that child has always found life difficult, or perhaps because she reminds the mother of herself when she was young. Whatever the background, jealousy will emerge when love is distributed unequally between the children in a family. If you do have a 'favourite', don't let it show, either by your words or by your actions.

Sharing

Case study: Fran is nine years old. She has a brother, Jim, who is six and a sister, Jennifer, who is five. The children love each other as much as would be expected in any family, but they have constant arguments when it comes to sharing toys, sweets and books. Each night, without fail, there are complaints about how Fran has pinched Jim's toy, or how Jennifer was given the most sweets. Their parents are totally fed up with this jealous behaviour and deal with the situation by laying down strict conditions, such as 'No sweets for anyone if you can't agree who gets what', 'You'll all go to bed if I hear one more argument about who sits in which chair', or 'I'll throw these toys out if you start fighting about whose turn it is to play with them'. The children appear to listen to these injunctions seriously – then immediately start fighting again. Even when backed up by punishments, the parental admonitions seem to have no effect. What would you do to help the children cope with their jealousy? Do you think the parents are handling the children appropriately?

Analysis: Sharing has to be taught. The tendency for children to be jealous about their possessions seems to be more natural than the tendency to share. The parents are attempting to control their children's jealousy mainly by the use of threats, supported by punishment in some instances. They could, however, try an alternative form of management. First, they could explain to the children what the benefits of sharing would be, rather than warning them of the dangers if they don't share. Second, they could reward the children when they do manage to share their toys without arguments, by allowing extra playing time before they have to go to bed. And third, they could show the children by example, letting them see that their mother and father are able to share out their possessions, to take turns choosing the television programme to be watched, and so on. These positive measures will have more effect than the punitive measures employed so far.

Coping with jealousy

A child has to learn to cope with her feelings of jealousy. She has to develop a way of keeping these natural – but unpleasant – emotions under control so that her enjoyment of life is not impaired. You can help your child achieve this in the following ways:

- *don't make your child feel guilty about being jealous.* Remarks such as 'You should be ashamed of being jealous of your brother' or 'Only horrible children get jealous' simply encourages the child to conceal her true feelings from you. It is also likely to produce a poor self-image, in that the child will begin to see herself in negative terms.
- *let the child know you understand what it is like to be jealous of someone else.* There is no harm in admitting to her that you also feel jealous at times, as long as you add that you don't let these feelings upset you or spoil your enjoyment of anything. The child's distress will ease once she realizes she can share her anxieties with you.
- *encourage your child to talk about her jealousy.* Voicing her feelings of jealousy will help her cope with them. Certainly, it is better than concealing them. Pretending that feelings of jealousy do not exist will not make them go away.

Jealousy

- *accept that children vary in the amount of jealousy they experience.* Some children are more sensitive than others and tend to react more strongly to situations that may lead to jealousy. The fact that your older child seems unaffected by jealousy does not mean your younger child will follow a similar pattern. Avoid comparing your jealous child with other children who appear to be less jealous since that may well make her even more jealous.
- *remember that very intense jealousy can be a sign of a child's deeper anxieties.* Where a child's jealousy manifests itself constantly at all times of the day, the emotion may be a sign of insecurity and lack of confidence. Parents should try to identify the underlying cause in such circumstances.
- *don't be surprised at the amount of jealousy and selfishness shown by young children.* Many psychologists take the view that children are instinctively selfish and possessive, and that development to some extent involves the child's moving away from thinking only about herself to thinking and caring about others. Therefore jealousy is shown by every child, to a greater or lesser extent.

Fairness doesn't mean equality

Treating your children fairly does not mean that you should treat them equally. Each child is an individual with her own particular emotional needs, and each child needs love and attention in varying amounts and in different ways. The idea that the best way of raising children is to treat then identically, by giving them all the same material items (when one child gets a toy, the others get the same toy) or giving them all the same opportunities (one gets skating lessons so the others will get skating lessons) is not an effective way of reducing jealousy. Of course, it is tempting to buy each of your children the same toy because that way there can be no complaints about one getting something better than the other. But it also means that one of the children will be getting something she doesn't really want. This tactic takes no account of each child's individuality. A child has to learn to accept there are differences between people. If her parents avoid that issue and pander to her jealousy every time, the child will not develop any control over her feelings.

Even where the parents adopt a policy of equal treatment, the children will find the outside world takes a different approach. Schools, for instance, encourage children to progress at their own pace. Children's clubs, whether sporting organizations or the Brownies, encourage each child to develop mastery in different areas, depending on the individual child's skills. These individual differences make life interesting, and are nothing a child need be afraid of. The child who lives in an environment that tries to create equality in everything will receive an abrupt jolt when she ventures beyond the family home.

Fairness is different from equality and reduces the possibility of jealousy between children. Fairness means taking a child's individual needs into account. One child might need lots of cuddles before going out to school in the morning, while her brother might simply prefer a smile from his parents. Each child in that family has different emotional needs and the parents meet these individual needs even though that results in the children being treated differently. But there will be very little jealousy between them. Differential treatment and preferential treatment are not the same.

Chapter 8

Fears in Childhood

Childhood fears are a normal part of early development. Psychological surveys confirm that up to 90 per cent of young children experience some form of mild fear in the pre-school years. These fears may be based on real events, such as fear of thunder and lightning, or on imagined things, such as fear of ghosts. Childhood fears – just like adult fears – do not have to be rational, and indeed few children can explain the basis of their worries. However, most childhood fears are due to temporary feelings of insecurity, which usually arise from the child's lack of understanding and control of the world around him.

When fears emerge

A child first shows signs of fear at around one year, perhaps in the form of thumb-sucking, hair-pulling, crying, stamping feet, and so on. (Bear in mind though that these same actions can be caused by other emotions as well.) Children at that age often become afraid when confronted by a new situation without their mother beside them. Distress in the mother's absence or when the mother leaves is a sign of a normal, close mother–infant relationship. One-year-olds will also show momentary fear when they experience loud noises, flashes of light, sudden movements, and strangers. The fear passes quickly when the frightening event is no longer visible or audible.

Understanding Children

By the age of two a child has a greater understanding and awareness of the world around him. Yet his understanding is not so great that he can fully explain everything that goes on around him. The combination of this partial understanding of the world and his lively imagination can produce fears of virtually anything. For instance, a toddler knows that spiders crawl all over the place because he sees that happening every few days. But he may not know that spiders do not eat children. The child's limited knowledge of the environment mixed with his imagination can result in a fear of spiders. In fact, fear of animals is particularly common in two-year-old children.

Between the ages of two and five years, fears of people, of objects, and of the unusual tend to decline in intensity. These are replaced by fears of anticipated events, imaginary events and even 'supernatural' events. Emotions seem to rule over the intellect at this age. Yet some fears are sensible and prevent the child from entering potentially hazardous situations. A fear of strangers is a healthy reaction because it stops the child from going away with someone he does not know. (This is discussed in more detail in Chapter 10.) Similarly, a fear of being injured by traffic encourages a child to learn road safety.

An older child tends to have fears that arise out of first-hand experiences of a hazardous event, such as a fear of dogs following a dog-bite, or a fear of fires following a dangerous fire in the house. At this age there are also fears that have a symbolic quality, for example fears of the dark, and fears of ghosts. One psychological study found that children are only moderately afraid of possible dangers (like being knocked down by a car) and yet are strongly afraid of almost impossible hazards (like being eaten by a wild lion).

Adults can cause fears

Parents use language differently from children. What may seem a casual remark to an adult may be perceived as something much more serious when heard by a child. A grandparent's simple comment, 'I hope I'm still alive when you have your next birthday', can have a dramatic effect on a young listener. He may take the words seriously and become concerned about the possibility of death. The same can happen when a child overhears parts of television or radio programmes, or snatches of adult conversation.

Of course, children need to be made aware of the routine hazards of domestic life, in the interests of safety. Electric room-heaters can catch fire, people can fall off ladders or trip down stairs, burglars can break into houses at night when the occupants are asleep, babies can drown in only two inches of bath water, and so on. These are real dangers. But they have to be kept in perspective. Continual reminders of what could happen may make a child afraid rather than cautious, and that is not the aim of safety warnings.

Eliminating fears

Some children do grow out of their fears without any help from their parents, but when the fear lasts for more than a few weeks then it probably means the child does need your support. In that situation, the following list of 'dos' and 'don'ts' applies:

DO

- *treat the fear seriously:* what may seem like a silly event to you may seem like an impending disaster in the eyes of your child. The child will not want to discuss his feelings with you unless he feels you are treating him seriously. That doesn't mean you should agree with what he says, but it does mean you should be prepared to listen to what he tells you, no matter how irrational the fear might seem.

- *ascertain the focus of the fear:* find out exactly what it is that your child is afraid of. Your child initially may not be able to say exactly what frightens him, but if you gently question him you may get more accurate information. For example, a child who becomes anxious when a cat approaches may be

Understanding Children

anxious about many different things. He could be afraid the cat will eat him, or that the animal's smell will rub off on him, or that he will get a ghastly disease from the cat. Through discussion you will be able to establish more precisely the area of his concern.

- *devise a series of interim goals that will lead your child eventually to the desired goal:* the final goal you want to achieve – which is the child's ability to cope with an event that previously terrified him – should be the end point of the process. You will have to decide on a series of 'stepping stones' leading to that. For instance, the first stage in overcoming a fear of cats might be for your child to let a cat come within twenty metres of him. The next stage might be for your child to let a cat come within ten metres of him. The last stage will be when your child can let a cat come up to him and stroke it without flinching.

- *tell the child what you are trying to achieve:* let him know that you want him to be able to overcome his fear of cats. Explain to him that you will want him to do this, that it is a shared venture between you. Each time you move from one stage to the next tell the child what your plans are, or else he may be frightened that you are going to push him too far, too soon. Your honesty with him will give him confidence.

- *encourage the child to associate calmness with each successive stage:* the technique for teaching this is straightforward. Stay with your child and let the cat approach within, say twenty metres (or whatever the next stage is). Your child's initial reaction will probably be tears, erratic breathing, and clutching you in terror. At that point encourage your child to be calm. Tell him he is safe, that he has nothing to worry about, that he doesn't need to be afraid of the cat. You may need to hold the child firmly so that he doesn't run away, but your constant reassurance will give him the confidence to get through this particular stage; he will have started to associate feelings of calmness with the idea of the cat coming close to him.

- *when one stage is mastered, move on to the next:* the child has mastered a stage when he is able to deal with it without becoming unduly afraid. When he is able to let a cat come within twenty metres without clinging to you, wanting you to be with him, crying, shaking or running away, then he is ready for the next stage. You may need three or four attempts spread over a week, at each stage, before your child is confident enough to cope.

- *repeat the process:* do this for each successive stage, allowing your child to build up his confidence. He will gradually realize that although he has not yet fully overcome his fear of cats he is well on the way. Your calmness and reassurance at each step are the best encouragement he can get.

- *tell your child what his reward will be each time the target is met:* let the child know what rewards you will give him whenever he takes one step closer to the desired goal. A few minutes' extra time playing before bed, an extra story read to him at night, or an extra trip to the park, can be effective incentives for him to continue with his efforts.

- *give lots of love and praise when the targets are met:* each time you see your child moving closer to being able to cope with his fear, give him lots of praise and cuddles. Tell him how well he's doing, how pleased you are with him. Again, that will increase his strength for the next stage of the procedure.

- *have realistic expectations of the child's progress:* you will not eradicate the child's fear overnight. The child is more likely to overcome his fear over a gradual period. Set a time scale of, say, eight weeks, during which time you hope to help your child overcome his particular fear, and work towards that.

DON'T

- *make fun of the child:* making light of the child's fears is counter-productive. While it is important that you give the child enough confidence to make him feel he will be able to overcome his fear, you shouldn't try to make the child feel foolish. That will not work. Comments like 'You are acting like a big baby' or 'I wish you would act your age; your friends aren't afraid of cats' will only increase your child's agitation.

- *bully your child:* this will not work either. Threatening a child who is afraid of cats with a smack if he doesn't pat the neighbour's animal is unlikely to be effective. In the short-term it might teach the child not to show his fear when you are with him, but in the long-term bullying doesn't teach the child any strategies for coping with the fear.

- *make allowances for your child's fears:* the worst thing you can do is to let the child alter his lifestyle so that his fear can be accommodated. While it is not helpful to throw the child in at the deep end, nor is it helpful to structure his life so that he avoids cats completely. Such a strategy makes the child feel his fear is justified and gives his active imagination a better opportunity to increase the fear.

- *let the child see you are upset by his fear:* the child who is afraid of something will often look to the adults with him to see how they are reacting. If the child sees you are agitated this will make him think he has good reason to be afraid, whereas if he sees you are calm then he will draw reassurance from that.

Nightmares

Nightmares occur most frequently in young children between the ages of four and six years, although research indicates that at least 25 per cent of children between the ages of six and twelve still have bad dreams. The occasional disturbed night is not a source of concern. Many different events can trigger off a bad dream. Some children always have nightmares when they eat particular foods late at night just before they go to sleep, such as cheese or chocolate. Other children have bad dreams whenever they watch adventure programmes on television prior to bedtime. These instances are normal, and the best way to avoid them is to avoid the stimulus that sets the child off. When your child does wake up distressed in the middle of the night, comfort him and stay with him until he is settled. Reassure him that was only a dream, that it didn't really happen, and that he is perfectly safe now. Your child may calm down quicker when you change the situation he is in. For instance, taking him to the toilet or downstairs for a drink of juice will help. Ill-health often affects a child's sleeping habits, and a sudden run of restless nights can be a warning that the child is about to develop an illness.

Repeated nightmares can be a sign of a child's deeper worries. Some fears only show themselves at night when the child is asleep. Freud suggested that children – like adults – are able to repress unpleasant feelings by pushing them into their unconscious. This 'defence mechanism', which protects the individual from distressing emotions, means that a child may be unaware of his true feelings while he is awake. These repressed fears may emerge at night when a child is asleep and cause the child to have nightmares. When bad dreams become a regular occurrence in a child's life, the parents should look closely at the child's circumstances to establish what it is that is troubling him.

Night terrors are an extreme form of nightmare, in which a child screams in his sleep and may even jump out of bed. The episode can last up to twenty minutes. When you go into the child's room, he may have his eyes wide open and yet still be convinced that he can see something frightening. Stay with your child and reassure him he is safe until he calms down. You will probably find that he can't remember anything about it the following morning. Night terrors are rare, but frightening both for the child who experiences them and for the parent who witnesses the child in a distressed state. As with nightmares, there is no cause for concern unless they become regular, in which case there will be something worrying him.

Phobias

Phobias are similar to normal childhood fears except that they are much more pervasive. Whereas a child with a fear of dogs will become anxious only when he actually comes in close proximity to one, a child with a phobia of dogs becomes anxious at the very thought of dogs, at a picture of a dog, or whenever someone mentions dogs in conversation. A phobia affects a child so much that it interferes with his whole life. To determine whether a fear is a harmless childhood phase or a phobia, ask yourself the following questions:

- *does the child show anxiety only when he experiences the dreaded event first hand?*
- *does the child's fear reaction pass as soon as he no longer is in contact with the object?*
- *is the child relaxed when he thinks about the feared event or sees it on television?*
- *is the child's life unaffected by the fear except when there is a first-hand encounter?*

If the answer to these questions is 'yes', then it is likely that your child's reaction is a normal childhood fear. It will pass as he grows older and more confident, and as long as you give him the appropriate help and support. If the answer to these questions is 'no', then his fear may have a deeper psychological significance, and merits closer consideration. The fearful behaviour may be a sign of the child's strong feelings of insecurity. Fortunately, genuine phobias are not common in childhood, but when they do occur professional psychological advice may be necessary to help the child overcome the difficulty.

Chapter 9

Birth Order and Personality

Psychological research indicates that birth order can be a significant influence on the way a child's personality develops. A great many studies have compared children of different birth orders, in terms of personality, intelligence, creativeness and independence. The results show clear differences between first-born children, second children and youngest children. Some of these psychological investigations have been very substantial. In 1974, a group of psychologists in Holland measured the intelligence of 400,000 men, and found that on average first-borns have a higher level of intelligence than those born later.

Bear in mind, though, every child is an individual. The fact that a baby is a first-born child, a second child, or whatever, does not mean she inevitably will develop the typical characteristics of that birth order. Rather, she will have a tendency to develop them. If you don't want your child to be heavily influenced by birth order, then there is a lot you can do. First, though, let's consider the main psychological findings.

The first-born child

You make most of your mistakes, as parents, with the first-born child. The first time the baby is held in your arms, you are a little bit nervous. Then there is all the paraphernalia of babyhood, like learning to change nappies, what creams to use to soothe the infant's bottom, how you make up feeds, how you establish regular sleeping patterns, what toys you should buy to stimulate the baby's interest, the medicine most suitable for the child's coughs, and so on. The first-born child is the guinea-pig of the family, the child on whom the mother and father learn about parenting – and on whom they make most of their mistakes. Fortunately, any 'errors' in child-care are usually put right by the time brothers and sisters are born.

First-born children (when compared to other children):

- have greater achievement in education and employment; they strive to meet academic goals, and find serious-minded activities challenging
- are more intelligent; one study of nearly half a million young males indicated that first-borns have the highest levels of intelligence among all the children in the family
- lack confidence and are less able to cope with anxiety, despite their success and higher intellectual skills; they are dependent on others, especially in times of stress
- are more conformist, more socially responsible; they are likely to dress conventionally, enjoying traditional hobbies and pastimes
- are more prone to emotional disorders; a higher proportion of first-born adults require psychotherapy than does any other birth order.

The first-born child, although having apparent advantages, remains a vulnerable, sensitive child. This happens because a first-born child is in the unique position of being an only child for some time then has to cope with the trauma of a newborn baby in the family.

Look at it from the first-born child's point of view. Her parents spend all their time with her, she gets lots of presents, and aunts, uncles, and grandparents fight for her love. Then adults around her start talking about a new baby coming in the family. The mother is preoccupied with her changing physical condition. A feeling of insecurity can quickly settle in. We, as adults, are well aware that loving a second infant does not decrease your love for the first. But the older child does not know that. She has to learn by experience – and that takes time.

Preparing the first-born child for the new arrival

The first rule of thumb is . . . prepare the first-born for the impending arrival of a brother or a sister. Don't wait until the last moment when the contractions are every two minutes. Start introducing the idea of the baby as soon as the physical signs of pregnancy become noticeable. Talking about the event well in advance lets the first-born express any anxieties she has.

When the child visits her new brother or sister in hospital for the first time, make sure the baby has a present for her (one you took into hospital with you). Let the first-born take a present for the new arrival. Of course, this exchange of gifts is artificial. Yet it can help form an emotional attachment between the two children right from the start. You should expect the first-born child to feel jealous, and this can be shown in many different ways. She could become aggressive to her parents, she could start being very clinging and afraid to let her father out of her sight, or she may regress and become babyish herself. These reactions are natural. Rejection of the child because she starts to behave appallingly will confirm her fears that her parents love her less than the new baby.

The best way to help the first-born relate to the baby is to involve her in the practicalities of baby-care. Let her fetch the nappies out of the cupboard, or throw away the dirty cotton-wool in the bin. Even a toddler is able to do something to help. Most times you will probably be so tired that you want to do everything yourself, since it is quicker that way. Resist that temptation and let the first-born child feel useful. No matter how small the task is, it will make her feel she is important.

The second child

By the time the second child comes along, as parents you are much more confident and experienced. The silly little things you used to lose sleep over – such as whether three layers of clothing are enough to keep the baby warm, or whether the squeaky toy was more suitable than the rattle – no longer enter your thoughts. This leads to a calmer atmosphere in the house. But this is offset by the fact that two children take up a lot more of your time and attention than one child does. Each child has to compete for attention now. So to that extent the second child has a tougher start to life than the first-born. But it probably makes her a little hardier.

Second children (when compared to other children):

- do less well in life than expected; second children are far less concerned with achieving success
- are less conformist and follow anti-establishment trends; for example, over 90 per cent of all scientists who supported Darwin's radical theory of evolution when it was first proposed were second or youngest children
- as adults, are very easygoing, gentle and cheerful, perhaps because they are less anxious and less concerned with achievements
- prefer non-academic activities; sports, music and art are their favourite pastimes.

A sense of rivalry often exists between second and first children, especially if the achievements of the first-born child are constantly paraded in front of the second child. This can happen at school, when the younger child has the same teacher as her older brother or sister. The older child can be a hard act to follow, particularly when she has been very successful academically. However, comparisons like that serve no purpose, and should be avoided at all costs. The second child's tendency towards the unconventional may be a reaction against the highly valued successes of her conventional older brother or sister.

Parental attitudes differ towards each child as well, and that can play a part. The experiences of raising the first child in the family gives parents confidence in their own abilities as mother and father. That feeling of being capable allows the parents to become more flexible with rules. Consequently, most second children are allowed more freedom than first-born children. This may be one explanation for the second child's less traditional and more creative nature.

Youngest children

Youngest children fluctuate between being the centre of attention – older brothers and sisters, aged five or six and upwards, often dote on a new baby – and having to fight for their rights. Parents have to make a specific point of making sure the youngest child does not get swept away in the tide of the older children, while at the same time ensuring the older ones don't 'spoil' her.

Youngest children (when compared to other children):

- are the most confident children of all; it seems that the hustle and bustle of family life helps youngest children cope easily with new situations
- handle their worries on their own; whereas children of other birth orders like to share their worries with someone else, youngest children deal with pressure themselves
- if male, tend to have more native cunning than their older brothers and sisters – hardly surprising, since if they didn't have guile they would always be last in line for everything
- if female, are less concerned about their physical appearance than are their older sisters; make-up and clothes are less important to women who are the youngest in their family.

Twins

There are so many popular myths about twins that it is difficult to separate fact from fiction. History tells us that some primitive tribes abandoned twins – or even murdered them – at birth because they believed one of the children had a demon father. The tribesmen were unable to determine which twin it was and so they played safe by disposing of both. This idea of the good twin and the bad twin is often expressed in popular culture. James Dean played the role of a very nasty twin in the film version of *East of Eden*. In contrast, the cinema can also present identical twins in a very romantic way, in which the children secretly swap places in life. Hayley Mills's portrayal of the identical daughters in *The Parent Trap* used this technique very effectively.

There is a widely held view that twins have a special psychic relationship which allows them to be constantly aware of the other's thoughts. Although there is no scientific evidence to support this idea, research has shown that twins often fabricate a secret language for talking exclusively between themselves. The children tend to give up this form of communication before they reach school age. But the existence of a special language between children is not unique to twins. Parents of non-twins often find their two pre-school children are able to communicate using terms adults cannot understand.

What is fact, rather than fiction, is that:

- approximately one pregnancy in eighty results in twins.
- twins tend to 'run' in families, and so a woman who is herself a twin, or has a twin relative, is more likely to give birth to twins than is a woman who has no twins in her family.
- women who conceive after the age of forty are four times more likely to produce twins than are women who conceive at the age of twenty.
- it is quite usual for the birth of twins to follow the birth of a single child.
- doctors are able to diagnose twins by the sixteenth week of pregnancy.
- most twins are born prematurely and are underweight.

Research evidence also shows that even identical twins are not exactly the same in every way. While it is true that identical twins have a greater similarity in heartbeat and pulse rate than do non-identical twins, clear differences often emerge. Parents frequently find that one identical twin is left-handed and the other is right-handed. The left-handed child is also likely to be the smaller twin. Twins often have different handwriting styles, and there are likely to be personality differences as well.

Twins (when compared to other children):

- are more likely to have speech problems
- tend to be more confident because each child has a constant companion right from the start of life; this encourages a feeling of security
- are able to share things more easily, simply because they learn this from the earliest days.

Although being a twin does have these effects on subsequent personality development, the actual birth order of the twins – that is, who emerged from the womb a few minutes before the other – does not matter. Yet people are fascinated by the birth order of twins, especially if the twins are identical. It helps adults sort out some way of distinguishing between the two look-alikes. The inherent danger in this type of artificial labelling – particularly when started by the children's parents – is rivalry and favouritism. The so-called older child may feel obliged to be a leader even if she would prefer not to be. Or she may feel inadequate if the younger twin develops faster.

Parents may be unsure whether to emphasize the twin's similarities or their differences. But the fact is that each twin will develop individually no matter what you do. Parents who force their children to act like two peas in a pod will cause unnecessary strain within the family. You may be tempted to give one twin a present every time the other twin is given one, and you may even be able to sustain that arrangement inside the home. But the children will have an abrupt surprise when they realize the outside world is not like that. The earlier that twins gain a sense of individuality the better. Discipline should also be dispensed individually since what suits one child may not suit the other. Each child has her own personality, requiring individual reactions from her parents.

You will have to choose whether to have both children in the same class, at nursery or at school, or whether to separate them at that stage. Separation can make the start to nursery or school that bit more stressful since the child will have to cope on her own without the support of her twin, but this disadvantage may be offset by the child's being allowed to establish her own unique identity. Separate classes make comparisons less likely, although you may believe that competition between your twins is healthy. Certainly, decisions about schooling should be well thought-out in advance.

The only child

Even though the tendency nowadays is towards smaller families, the single-child family is still not the norm. Some say that too much fuss is made about a child's not having any brothers or sisters, and claim that only children are the same as first-born children. The main difference, however, is that only children never have to compete with anyone else for their parents' attention. They never have to wait their turn in a queue of brothers and sisters, and they never have to share their toys. That is quite an advantage. On the other hand, life can be lonely for the only child.

Only children (when compared to other children):

- are more self-interested; these children have only themselves to think about and expect to get their own way
- need approval from authority figures; this extends into adulthood where many only-child employees rely heavily on the approval of their managers
- relate better to older people; being raised in the company of adults makes them feel comfortable with more mature individuals

- make better leaders, and can be a tremendous asset in situations where initiative is needed.

The cliché that the only child is selfish and over-indulged is not always accurate. However, if you find your child developing these characteristics, concentrate on the following strategies. First, encourage the child to share her toys with friends, neighbours and classmates. Try to involve her in team games. Nurseries and playgroups are good places for organizing games that require sharing. Second, help the child relate to children her own age. The best way of doing this is to send her to playgroup or nursery, but if you can't manage to do that, then invite other children round to the house for her to play with. When the only child is in the company of other children, discourage her from making excessive demands for attention from the adults. Third, some only children expect everything to be done for them. As parents, you have to encourage the child to take more control over life's everyday events. This can apply to any activity, including washing, dressing, feeding and tidying up. Lastly, the only child is used to being the centre of attention. Learning to share adult time with others is not easy, so create opportunities to break this pattern, for example, by playing games where the children have to take turns, or by having small group discussions where every child is given a chance to speak.

Other factors

There are other factors to take into account when considering the importance of birth order. The age-gap between children matters. If there is, say, a ten-year difference between the first child and the second child, then the younger will probably be treated as a first-born even though she has an older brother or sister, whereas the youngest child in a family in which children are born every eleven months is going to have to struggle to get individual attention. Then there are economic factors. Some psychologists attribute the greater educational achievements of the first-born child and the only child to financial advantage. The parents are able to concentrate their resources on one child. Yet the reverse may happen. Many parents find their income drops with the arrival of the first child, but by the time the third child is born the family income has risen again. In these families, there is more disposable income to meet the needs of the youngest child than there was to meet the needs of the first. Assessing the true effect of birth order is a complicated business.

Possibilities or probabilities?

Despite these personality trends in birth order, every one of us can think of people we know who are exceptions to these typical birth-order profiles, which confirms that virtually all the characteristics discussed in this chapter, for all the different birth orders, can be counterbalanced by thoughtful parental behaviour. If you are concerned that your children may be unduly influenced by birth order, then:

- *make a special point of allocating individual time to each child in the family*. In a family of two parents, and perhaps three children, it is not easy to spend time with each child on its own. Yet your special effort to do this reminds the child that she is an individual.
- *give equal encouragement to all your children*. It is easy to slip into the habit of diminishing enthusiasm for each successive child's achievements. Your youngest child's first reading book may not carry the same magical excitement for you as your oldest child's first reading book did. But the youngest child has to feel that you care as much about her achievements as those of the older children.
- *don't demean the youngest child's academic attainments with tales of how well the older children managed when they were in that class*. You may be tempted to use that tactic to encourage a younger child who is struggling in school – it will only discourage her further.
- *ensure that all your children share responsibility*. The oldest child does not have to be held responsible for the misdemeanours

of the younger children when they are playing outdoors. The younger child is just as capable of tidying away her toys as the oldest child is.

- *give every child – whether first-born, second or youngest – her proper place in the family.* Every child deserves to be loved and respected in her own right.
- *remember that sensitive handling by parents is the most influential factor of all in a child's development.* The way parents deal with circumstances like birth order is more crucial than the circumstances themselves.

Chapter 10

Shyness

Every child is shy sometimes. Even the most vivacious, talkative child can 'dry up' when he feels overwhelmed by the novelty of an unfamiliar situation. This reaction is normal.

Shyness changes with age

Parents take great pride in introducing their child to other adults, and it can be extremely embarrassing if your child acts uncharacteristically shyly on such occasions. However, you should have realistic expectations. Much depends on how old the child is. Although every child matures at a different rate, the following approximate age guidelines apply to most children:

- *one week old:* a newborn baby cannot differentiate one person from another and therefore does not show any signs of shyness. While it is true that some babies will take a feed from only one person in particular and not from anyone else, most babies will happily interact with anyone who shows them kindness and interest.
- *six months old:* by this age the infant has begun to differentiate familiar faces from unfamiliar faces. The six-month-old infant is able to recognize the people closest to him, his parents, his brothers and sisters. He will probably be shy of strangers, no longer friendly to anyone and everyone. This phase of shyness usually means that he cries when a stranger

becomes too attentive to him. The six-month-old infant may not want to leave his mother's knee when there is a stranger close by. Medical examinations at this age often prove to be trying for all concerned because of this.

- *one year:* the child now has greater awareness of who is familiar and who is not. He still remains shy, however, and may cling to his parents when they take him into new situations. The child may even cover his eyes with his hands or arms when a stranger approaches, or try to hide himself behind his parent. A child of this age taken to a mother–and–toddler group often sits 'glued' to his mother, desperately keen to join in the fun and games yet at the same time not secure enough to leave his mother for an independent foray into the playroom.
- *two years:* a child of this age has a greater degree of self-confidence, but may still hesitate to talk to people he doesn't know. A stranger is more likely to be greeted with silence rather than tears. Because the two-year-old is able to walk, he now can remove himself physically from any situation he doesn't like – when he feels shy of anyone he simply runs out of the room.
- *three years:* many children of this age are confident enough to accept attention from children and adults they do not know well – albeit, cautiously. The typical three-year-old is a combination of increased self-assuredness and decreased shyness, which means he is more able to cope with meeting new children and adults. Playgroups are well suited to the social needs of a child this age, and most three-year-old children enjoy playing with other children of their own age. They do not feel the need to have their mother with them all the time.
- *five years:* most of the earlier signs of shyness have gone, partly due to the increased confidence that comes with growing up, and partly due to the experience of social encounters in the earlier years. Even so, the child of five may still show shyness when the situation is totally new. Parents often find, for instance, that the first day of primary school stuns their child into shyness – but that passes quickly.

- *the older child:* from about the age of five upwards, a child will be able to talk about his shyness, and may be able to say what it is that causes him to feel embarrassed on certain occasions. Although his explanations may not be exact, he will have some insight into his feelings. This expressive ability can be helpful for parents trying to understand their shy child because what may appear disconcerting for adults may not be the factor that upsets a child. So ask your older child what it is about the social encounter that makes him feel uneasy. You will probably find he wants to talk about it, and your attentiveness to his shyness will encourage him to be more confident the next time.

Shyness can be a safeguard

There are many circumstances in which shyness is a healthy response – one which protects a child from danger. The shy child who will not go off in a car with a total stranger is behaving more sensibly than the talkative child who is prepared to go away with anyone who is friendly towards him. Shy or not, children have to be taught the danger of strangers. It is ironic that parents have to tell their child to be wary of strangers just at the time when the child's confidence is strong enough to cope with unfamiliar adults. But it needs to be done.

Explain to your child why he should not talk to strangers. Tell him that not all adults are kind to children and that he cannot tell who is a kind person and who is nasty just by looking at them. You don't need to go into all the gory details of child assault, but you do want him to realize the seriousness of what you are saying. It is best to lay down very clear guidelines for your child. Make it simple – 'Don't talk to any stranger at all, no matter what he says to you.' Even a three- and four-year-old will appreciate that directive from you when it is accompanied by a reasonable explanation. You should also add that he should not accept sweets from people he doesn't know.

Having laid down these rules to your child, he may then

sensibly ask what he should do if he gets lost. Tell him to ask for help from any person in a uniform or to ask help from a woman. Of course, that is no guarantee he will be safe, but it does increase his chances of coming into the temporary safekeeping of a benign adult.

Privacy

Parents sometimes confuse a child's desire for privacy with shyness. A child is entitled to privacy, and may be guarded and shy, even in his parents' presence, when an adult known to his mother and father but not to himself smothers him with hugs and kisses. This frequently happens at those once-a-year family gatherings when aunts and uncles see their nephews and nieces after an interval of several months. The child may have no recollection of having met these relatives before, and shyness in that situation is normal. No adult would like a total stranger to rush up to him in the middle of the street and embrace him, so it is unreasonable to expect a child to like that either. Respect your child's right to privacy. Everybody has to feel comfortable in a person's presence before physical affection is acceptable. Children are no exceptions.

Strategies for overcoming shyness

The best way of dealing with most shy children is to let them interact in their own time, or perhaps to give them sensitive encouragement to mix with other children. Although shyness is a passing phase for most children, there are some children who retain their shyness longer than others their own age. In fact, some people remain shy all their lives. That does not mean they are inadequate or even that they are unhappy. But the shy person does find socializing a hurdle, and from that point of view parents may want to help their child become more outgoing. If you are in that situation try the following strategies for helping your child cope better with social encounters:

Understanding Children

- *build up your child's self-confidence:* the shy child's embarrassment stems from his lack of confidence in his own abilities. You have to encourage the child to feel that he is as competent and capable as any other child he meets. Discuss his strong points with him, for example, that he is good at singing, or that he is kind. Emphasize these positive attributes, stressing all the time that these features will make other children like him.
- *give your child lots of social experiences:* you cannot reasonably expect your shy child to become outgoing unless he has plenty of opportunities to mix with other children. Make sure he plays with children his own age. Invite other children to your house to play with your child, and take him to playgroup or nursery, depending on his age. As long as there is a variety of social situations in which he can interact with other children, then his shyness should disappear eventually.
- *don't let your shy child avoid people:* the shy child would much rather be on his own, and it becomes easy for you to allow him to decline invitations simply because you know the trouble the child is likely to cause when he gets there. Yet the more you let him back away from social encounters then the more entrenched he will become in his shyness.
- *encourage your child to think of the other person:* shy children, and adults, usually spend the first few moments of social encounters thinking about themselves. Your child might be wondering about his appearance, about whether the other child likes him or not, about whether he will be able to keep track of his toys, and other self-centred thoughts. So encourage your child to focus on the other child, to imagine what he is thinking and feeling. Your child will find the first few moments of any meeting a lot easier if he adopts this strategy.
- *teach your child opening strategies:* the first few moments in any meeting are the most difficult, and much of the tension eases after that. The shy child may find the uncertainty of what to do in these initial seconds is what troubles him most, and therefore you should teach him specific strategies

for use when he meets new people. Be quite specific in your advice; for instance, tell your child that he should ask the other child to play a game, or that he should ask the other child about his favourite television programmes, or that he should ask the child to play with his colouring books and crayons. The actual opening move itself does not matter. What does matter is that your child has something definite to do in the first few crucial moments.
- *practice:* let your child practise these strategies in role-play situations in the comfort and security of his own home. A young child enjoys make-believe games and will be comfortable 'pretending' to meet people. Your guidance through role-play will help him gain confidence. The role-play situations could be shopping, talking to other children at playgroup or nursery, or answering the telephone. Teach your child how he should react and then act it out, rather like the way he might rehearse lines from a play. This way he will learn how to cope without having the embarrassment of making mistakes in front of other people in the process.

Physical deformity

A child with a visible deformity has to cope with a particular problem. It is not just that this child feels different from other children – he is different. And this can create shyness. Children hate to be different. Whether the difference is a facial deformity, an unsightly birthmark, a physical disability affecting the way the child walks, or a cleft palate, the psychological impact can be significant. A child's self-image is affected by the way people react to him, and so what starts out as a minor physical problem can quickly assume astronomic proportions when other children start to draw attention to it. Children are by nature inquisitive and are likely to question the child about the deformity. These questions – born out of curiosity rather than malice – can push the recipient into a wall of shyness.

Try to anticipate the behaviour of the other children. Where a child has a physical deformity, prepare him for the glances and enquiries that he is likely to receive when he ventures out of the house. Explain that everyone is different, that no two people are the same. Emphasize to your child that his physical defect is slight in comparison to all his good qualities. And reiterate that well-worn cliché that other children will stop teasing him once they realize the teasing has no effect. A little advance preparation will help your child deal with the real thing when it arises.

When shyness becomes a problem

Shyness can be a worrying sign when it suddenly appears in a child who was previously confident and outgoing. The onset of uncharacteristic shyness can be an indication that the child feels insecure. If that happens with your child – and remember it is the change to a state of shyness that is important, not the shyness itself – you should look closely at his circumstances to discover what is worrying him. It may be a problem at home, or with his friends. Shyness of this sort is usually a symptom of deeper worry and it is the deeper worry that requires attention. Seek professional advice if necessary.

Chapter 11

Separation and Divorce

Arguments are often part of normal married life, and can provide a useful way of releasing tension. Nobody enjoys a heated exchange of words, but sometimes that is the only way couples can clarify misunderstandings between them. With some couples, however, arguments are symptomatic of a much deeper difficulty, and for these partners the end point is separation or divorce. At least one marriage in three finishes in divorce. Consequently over a third of all children born in the last decade will spend some time living in the home of a single parent. Even if parental disharmony does not lead to divorce, there may be periods of temporary separation, or perhaps continual rowing between the mother and father. Whatever the final outcome of the animosity, a child in that family is at risk emotionally.

Marriage under stress

A child will be aware of any prolonged tension between her parents, even when the family stays together. Some parents claim that although there is no love between them any more, their children are unaware of the true feelings existing between them. These parents believe that since they have not openly flaunted their disagreements at home then their children are oblivious to it all. These beliefs are based more on hope than on reality. A child is just as able to interpret non-spoken signs of ill-feeling as she is to interpret language.

Although her parents may not have exchanged words in temper in front of the child they will have revealed their emotions in other ways. Long silences at mealtimes, lack of loving responses between the father and mother and a subdued family atmosphere all tell a child that something is wrong between her parents. Parental tension cannot be hidden completely.

Build-up to divorce

Research has shown that children are influenced more by family discord than by the actual break-up of the family, if that happens. The build-up to a parental split seems to create more psychological damage in children than the split itself. This is probably because many couples have a lengthy period of dispute before making the enormous decision to separate. Quite rightly, the couple will try hard to maintain the family as it is, so there may be a phase of several years in which the tensions in the parental relationship continue until they are either resolved or else the relationship eventually breaks down. In the latter case, the decision to terminate the marriage usually has the effect of removing hositility from the home environment. Of course, the child then has to readjust to living with one parent only. But uncertainties have been removed. Some children find that easier to cope with than living in a house where there is constant rowing.

Parental tensions

Most relationships have areas of tension, and marriage is no exception. Young children seem to be particularly sensitive to the following sources of conflict between their parents:

- dissatisfaction with sexual relationships
- where one partner feels neglected by the other
- when emotions are not freely expressed
- when one partner feels dominated by the other.

If you find that you have conflict with your partner over any of these issues, treat them as high priorities, since your children are likely to be affected. Not all couples are able to resolve relationship difficulties on their own. The Marriage Guidance Council (now known as Relate) can be a useful resource.

Why children are affected

Children are affected by parental separation or divorce for several reasons. First, a child needs to experience stable family relationships in the developing years since these act as a base for her future social relationships. Failure to form at least one firm emotional connection with an adult in the first three years of life can have long-term detrimental effects on later personality development. Parents find it hard to give their children all the necessary love and attention when they themselves are struggling to cope with life, and the child suffers as a result. The disruption of a marriage when the child is young is also likely to disrupt the parents' relationships with the child.

Second, a child will model a great deal of her behaviour on her parents. That doesn't mean that a child is a carbon copy of her mother and father, but there is a link between the two. In a marriage beset with rows and hostilities between the mother and father, the child is presented with a disturbed model of behaviour which she herself is likely to imitate in some ways. Third, parents who fight constantly about their own relationship are likely to use their children as a way of getting back at their partner. One parent may deliberately exercise different levels of control than the other one, for the sake of aggravating the partner. These conflicting demands only upset the child even further. Finally, every child wants to have both parents, and will do her best to remain loyal to both. This is extremely difficult to achieve.

How to tell the children

When discord is so severe that the parents do separate permanently, they face the difficult task of telling their children. There are many ways of doing this. The words parents use to inform their children depend very much on the individuals involved. They also depend on the openness that already exists within the family. Some parents take the view that conflict of any sort should never be expressed freely, and they discourage open discussions of ill-feeling. In that type of family the child has little experience of dealing with trauma. The impact of divorce can be more damaging because the child has not acquired skills for coping with crises. Other parents take the view that tensions should always be aired, not concealed. The child brought up in that environment is more likely to be able to cope with stress when it arises.

Parents will hesitate to tell their child about the divorce for fear of the child's reaction. They may be so afraid she becomes upset, or that she will feel it is all her fault, that they keep postponing the inevitable moment. Some parents never actually tell their child the true situation. Instead, they present other explanations for the fact they have separated, perhaps saying that the father has to work away from home for a while. However, this strategy of keeping the child in the dark about what is going on rarely works. The child has to be told at some point.

The best way of telling a child is to do so gradually, over a period of time, in a calm manner. This gives the child plenty of time to mull over the idea so that she can become steadily accustomed to it. Parents should explain to the child they don't get on with each other any more and that they have decided to live apart. But they should also emphasize that both parents still love her. The child may be worried that she will become unloved because her mother and father are separating. She needs reassurance that both parents will continue to care for her. Another worry a child in a broken home often has is that the divorce is somehow her fault. She sees relationships in more simplified ways than an adult, and may think it is her misbehaviour that has caused the separation. Parents have to reassure her about this as well.

Once the child is told, she will have lots of questions to ask about where she is going to live, how she is going to get to school, who will look after her, and what her friends will say when they hear. Each question should be dealt with as it arises. She should not be made to feel that she is annoying her parents by her enquiries. Through this question-and-answer process the child comes to terms with the reality of what is happening.

The reaction

All children will react adversely to parental separation and divorce. After all, one of the most important people in her life is leaving her. The child's initial reaction is likely to be one of total disbelief and inability to understand. The child may not be able to accept what you say to her. Some children will cry, while others will respond with silence. It depends on the particular child.

Once the news sinks in, the child may begin to show signs of emotional stress. Her behaviour may change in any number of ways, even though she is unaware why these changes are occurring. She could become:

- clinging to both parents
- withdrawn at school or nursery
- aggressive at home and towards her friends
- apathetic towards her school work
- restless, sleepless and irritable.

Any of these changes in the child's behaviour indicates a deeper emotional reaction to the divorce, stemming from the feeling of insecurity that the loss of a parent brings. If you find yourself in that situation, be patient with your child. Remember that she is not behaving this way just to be awkward – she cannot help it. Always expect an emotional reaction from your child. If she does cope well without showing signs of stress then regard that as an unexpected bonus. Fortunately, most reactions are only temporary. A child usually adapts in time to her new life as part of a one-parent family. Occasionally a child's distress does not ease with time. In such cases you should seek professional psychological help for your child.

The interim period

The first months immediately following the separation are the most unsettling time for all concerned. Both the adults and the children are emotionally vulnerable. Resist the temptation you may feel to over-indulge the child. Naturally you want to convey a feeling of love and security, but extreme indulgence as compensation for the child's distress will only make matters worse. The child needs stability at home, and needs to feel her remaining parent is in full control. A caring, firm discipline is the best form of management.

Amid the chaos that reigns after divorce, you may find your child playing off one parent against the other. Children are quick to exploit weaknesses in discipline and may use the temporary crisis to manipulate others in the family. The child may say that although her mother doesn't allow her sweets, when she is with her father she is allowed as many sweets as she wants. Or she may tell her father that her mother smacks her every night. Be wary of statements like that and don't immediately take them at face value. The only way to avoid that sort of manipulative behaviour is for both parents to set similar standards for behaviour. Some divorces are so bitter that the parents will not talk to each other, and it is hard to achieve uniformity of discipline in these circumstances. Failure to do so, however, only adds to the child's difficulties.

A child will not want to see open disagreements between her mother and father, whether the parents live together or not. Avoid open quarrelling in front of the children. And don't drag the children into your disputes. Irrespective of the rights and wrongs of the marital rows, the parents are still mother and father to the child and have to behave in a responsible and reasonable way.

Custody and access

There are many good reasons for children in disrupted families to maintain contact with the parent no longer living at home:

Separation and Divorce

- *fears:* a child may have unconscious fears that the estranged parent cannot manage on his own – contact with both parents helps reduce these fears.
- *responsibility:* a child may have periodic feelings of personal responsibility for the break-up – contact with both parents provides a balanced perspective.
- *stability:* separation has taken place and the child's world has been shattered – contact with both parents provides an element of stability.
- *love:* a child will continue to love both parents – lack of contact with the father or mother will cause the child unnecessary pain.

Evidence from psychological research confirms the positive value of maintaining contact with both parents. In 1980, a study of divorced families found that about a third of the children were coping well and had no emotional difficulties five years after the divorce, that about a third were coping reasonably well, and that the remainder were showing signs of emotional difficulties. The main difference between the 'copers' and the other two groups of children was that they saw both parents regularly. The children with emotional difficulties tended to be the ones who seldom, or never, saw one of their parents.

When making custody and access arrangements, try to reach a reasonable agreement with your ex-partner before you go to court. Don't ask the children what they would like to do since they are too young to be able to make that sort of decision. It is better to present the arrangements to them as a *fait accompli*. They will be pleased with whatever you arrange, as long as it means they can see both parents for some of the time. If you go into the courtroom full of indecision and bitterness towards each other, the judge (or sheriff, in Scotland) is likely to ask for a social welfare report before he makes a decision, and that will only postpone further any definite arrangement.

Access visits are very important for a child. They allow her to maintain contact with her estranged parent even though she is living with the other parent. Yet access visits can be unsettling at times for the child because they are a constant reminder to her that the parental separation is permanent. Access visits can also become unsettling when they are used by one parent to turn the child against the other, or when the child is used to 'spy' on the life of the ex-partner. Strategies like these place the child under unnecessary strain and should be avoided whatever the temptation.

Take access visits seriously. If you have to collect your child from your former spouse, then arrive at the agreed time and return your child back to her home at the agreed time. Likewise, if you have to get your child ready for a visit from your ex-partner, make sure you have her ready in plenty of time. Of course, these visits can be tense for everyone. But remember your child only wants these occasions to run smoothly, and it is in her best interests that they do so. Bickering between divorced parents will only increase the child's existing distress. On the other hand, continual and regular access will help the child cope with the traumatic effects of divorce.

After the divorce

In the long term, children from disrupted families are no more likely to be delinquents than are any other children. Nor are they more likely to present educational problems in schools. Nor are they more likely to have social difficulties. Most of the bad effects of divorce seem to lessen after a couple of years, once the family rebuilds itself and adjusts to the new circumstances. But the responsibility for carrying the family through the crisis rests with the parents, not the child. Any psychological damage as a result of parental separation will not be permanent if the adults act in a sensitive and reasonable way.

Chapter 12

Remarriage and Step-Parenting

Step-parenting becomes more common every year. As well as the many marriages that end in divorce, there are also marriages that terminate because of bereavement. The remarriage rate is now over 50 per cent higher than it was thirty years ago. Estimates suggest that almost three children out of ten are living with one natural parent and one step-parent, usually a step-father. Although not all remarriages are successful – the divorce rate for second marriages is still higher than the divorce rate for first marriages – the majority of these remarriages do work. This suggests that most people continue to perceive a family background as the best environment for raising a child despite their unhappy experiences from their first marriage.

Couples in a second marriage tend to experience different problems from those experienced by couples in a first marriage. Surveys have shown that difficulties in a first marriage most frequently stem from social and emotional immaturity, lack of readiness for marriage, and sexual dissatisfaction. Another major source of conflict in a first marriage is worry over money. Problems with children come bottom of the list. In contrast to this, the greatest area of conflict in a second marriage is management of the children. It is that issue which seems to occupy much of the couple's attention. This underlines the complexities of step-parenting, and confirms that many partners with children enter a second marriage without full realization of the pitfalls ahead of them.

Resolving old feelings

The parents should not expect their child to welcome the new marriage with open arms. They should not expect the child to be happy simply because he has a mother and father again. From the child's point of view, marriages are things that don't work. Experience has taught him that mothers and fathers don't stay together for ever. Therefore, the child is unlikely to relish what he sees as the prospect of living through another period with lots of arguments and ill-feeling. He has to learn to trust the stability of his new family, and this takes time and patience.

Before the child of a broken home will be able to accept the reality of a step-parent, he needs to resolve his feelings about the first marriage. Easier said than done, because the child may not have a clear understanding of what he feels. All he knows is that he isn't happy and that he misses his father. But he may not be able to articulate his emotions at a more sophisticated level than that. Parents in that situation should encourage their child to talk about his feelings. Don't be afraid of what he might say. The best way of resolving relationship difficulties is to express them openly.

Adjustment to remarriage

A child's adjustment to a remarriage, and his ability to integrate into the new family structure, depends on a number of factors:

- *acceptance of the previous loss:* a child may unconsciously deny that his parents have separated. This process of denial is a form of psychological protection and is a natural defensive reaction to unpleasant experiences. But step-parenting will not work until the child can accept that the previous marriage is over.
- *time between marriages:* there is no ideal time gap between a divorce and a remarriage. A short time span leaves children too little time to get over the trauma of divorce before

experiencing the impact of the new family. With many separations, there is a new partner already available at the time and often in these circumstances the adults think there is no need to wait. Yet the child may feel too rushed. It often comes down to a case of putting the child's happiness before the adults' happiness. Some parents, however, find that a long time gap between marriages is not the best solution either. A child gets used to having his single parent's full attention all to himself and he may become set in his ways. He may resist the idea of sharing his parent with someone else.

- *parental expectations:* the biggest mistake adults make in a second marriage is to underestimate their children's sensitivity and to expect too much from them. Parents often assume that the child will easily adjust to a remarriage. On this assumption, they do not spend enough time with the child discussing any anxieties he may have. Parental expectations must be realistic.
- *divided loyalties:* where the family break-up arises from divorce, a child really has three parents – the two natural parents and the step-parent. Like it or not, he has to learn to live with the idea of having a step-parent at home while one of his natural parents lives away. This needs careful handling by the adults. A child who is forced to choose between his step-parent and his natural parent will be distressed. Research shows that in many happy remarried families the child still sees his natural parent.
- *adult jealousy:* ex-spouses may be jealous when their former partner remarries. The temptation to use the child to get at the step-parent must be resisted, or else the child himself will suffer. A child is capable of having a good relationship with a step-parent and a natural parent at the same time. Each relationship contributes to the child's development in its own way.
- *the child's age:* under eights are less affected by parental remarriage than are older children. Although children of pre-school age cannot understand the full implications of remarriage, they are more able to adjust to their new

step-parent. Children of primary school age have greater awareness of their family circumstances, but have more difficulty accepting them. A child of this age often longs for the absent father, thereby impairing new relationships with the step-parent. Adolescence is the most difficult age of all for a child to adapt to remarriage. By this age he has already begun to establish his own independence and does not want to form new ties with anyone in his family.

- *assuming responsibilities:* many step-fathers are keen to take on their new role in parenthood, often failing to realize that this has to be a gradual process. Step-fathers tend to assume full parental responsibilities too soon, before the child is ready. This can cause an unnecessarily difficult start to their relationship.

Jealousy of other children

When a second marriage involves the amalgamation of two sets of children from two previous marriages, the scene is set for jealousy between the children. This is most marked when the children are of the same age. Each child feels threatened by the other children, lest the parental love for him diminishes. Both parents have to ensure divisions are not created and that all children receive their equal share of attention from both parents, especially in the early stages of the marriage. Activities should be organized as a unified family, with both parents and all the children participating. Alongside that, both parents should spend some time alone with each of the children, whether playing a game with them, talking to them, or going out for a walk. These actions help strengthen the bonds between the children and their step-parents.

When the second marriage produces a new baby, the existing children in the family might feel threatened and insecure. The parents should emphasize to all their children that their love for them is as strong as it ever was and that the arrival of a new baby won't change that. The rules for preparing a child for the new baby apply to this situation as well. (This is discussed in more detail in Chapter 9.) Some couples in a remarriage make a deliberate decision not to have any children of their own because of the detrimental effect this might have on the existing children. That is a personal decision and yet seems a rather drastic measure to take in order to avoid a potential pitfall. Every child adds a new and unique dimension to a family. Sensitive loving parenting will make all the children feel secure.

Relationships in the new family

The stereotyped view of the step-parent is someone who is wicked, uncaring and selfish, and who has very poor relationships with the step-children. This idea is promoted in children's literature with such stories as *Cinderella* and *Snow White*. Fortunately there is little basis in reality for this pessimistic view. Several studies on the effects of remarriage on children – involving thousands of step-families with at least one step-child – have found that:

- six out of ten families judged themselves to have excellent relationships between parents and children, and two stated they had good relationships. Only two families of the ten felt they had poor relationships between the step-children and the step-parents.
- the age of the step-mother at the time of remarriage was important. More step-mothers over the age of forty reported excellent relationships with their step-children than did women under that age. The age of the step-father was not found to be significant.
- nearly twice as many children under the age of thirteen had excellent relationships with their step-mother than did older children. Yet the age of the children had no effect on their relationship with their step-father.
- relationships between parents and children in step-families were found to be better when the couple had given birth to children of their own, as were relationships between the children themselves. A natural child in a step-family seemed to act as a binding force.
- relationships between step-parents and step-children were

usually satisfactory. Step-fathers are more likely to form close connections with their step-children than step-mothers, particularly if the step-child is male.

- step-fathers tend to be more competent in parenting skills than fathers in intact families, and seem well able to cope with raising step-children.
- the self-image of a child from a reconstituted family is no different from the self-image of a child in an original family. Being in a step-family does not adversely affect the way a child sees himself or the feelings of personal worth he has.
- children in one-parent families, where the father is absent, tend to have poorer educational achievements than children in intact families. However, the appearance of a step-father often reverses this pattern.
- working-class families appear to cope with remarriage better than middle-class families, probably because working-class families have a greater tendency to take friends and relations into their homes, and so are more prepared for sharing their families.
- women are better able to form good relationships with their step-children when they have their natural children living with them as well. This factor does not appear to influence a step-father's relationship with his step-children.
- step-families that arise out of bereavement have a higher level of satisfactory emotional relationships than step-families that arise out of divorce, largely because the child has not experienced a family life dogged by parental arguments.
- boys find it easier to become close to their step-father and to be more relaxed with him than girls do.

There is no research evidence to support the view that there are major differences between children living in their original families and children living in step-families. Children from step-families have similar emotional development to children from original families. True, step-families do tend to have an initial period in which feelings of tension and insecurity are stronger than in normal families, but this soon levels out –

and anyway, there are plenty of original families that have experienced difficult phases. In fact, boys who have stepfathers tend to be more socially independent than boys in original families.

All families face similar problems

Whether a child is in an intact family or in a restructured family, the parents' behaviour, the way discipline is presented and implemented in the family, the amount of conflict between the husband and wife, the relationships between the parents and their children, and the way love and affection are expressed are the factors that matter. Family relationships are much more important than family structures. There is absolutely no foundation for the belief that a child in a step-family is disadvantaged, or that he will be permanently damaged by the trauma of his first family's disruption. Young children are especially capable of adapting to their new circumstances, and are capable of forming new and satisfactory emotional connections with their step-parents. There are more difficulties when the child is older – but this applies to every family. A child will thrive when raised in any family with love and parental guidance, whether it is a first family or second family. Parents facing the decision of whether to remarry should not be influenced by erroneous expectations of failure. A remarriage is usually in the children's best interests.

Chapter 13

Independence

The first few years of life are characterized by two conflicting trends. On the one hand, the child becomes dependent on her parents for love and security, and this emotional connection with her parents gives her a strong psychological foundation for later life. On the other hand, the child also develops her natural tendencies to be independent. There is no specific age when a child should be independent, when she should be able to start doing things for herself. There are certain age-related milestones of independence which are important for all children, such as being able to sit up unaided, being able to walk, being able to have toilet control, and so on. But outside these obvious ones, much will depend on your own views as parents.

Parental attitudes

Psychologists have divided parental attitudes towards independence into three categories. The autocratic parent is described as one who gives the child no freedom to express her own ideas and feelings, who always makes decisions for the child, and who does not offer the child any explanation for household rules. The democratic parent is one who allows the child to participate in family decision-making, by letting her make many small decisions on her own, though at the same time retaining the final say in what the child can and cannot do. And the permissive parent is described as one who gives the child total freedom to do as she pleases, encouraging her to do what she wants, irrespective of the wishes of others.

Research studies comparing these three different styles of parental behaviour and their respective impact on the child's dependence have not surprisingly found that the child of democratic parents tends to be more independent than the child of either permissive parents or autocratic parents. And the more that parents offered their child explanations for rules of behaviour, then the greater was the child's level of independence.

Democratic parenting – coupled with regular explanations of why certain rules are adhered to in the family – encourages independence for several reasons. First, the child is provided with many supervised opportunities for testing her own ideas. This gives her a chance to think independently, while at the same time be protected from any inappropriate decisions she might make. Second, the child's confidence is increased because she feels loved and respected, instead of feeling either controlled or uncared for. Third, democratic parents themselves are usually independent-minded and so the child models herself on their own attitudes.

Encouraging independence

Training your child to be independent can be tiresome because of the demands it makes on you. But don't leave it all to chance. A planned approach along the following lines will give your independence training a clear structure:

- *decide what it is you want your child to achieve:* your goals have to be very specific so that you know precisely what to aim for. 'Going to a friend's party next week without her mother' is a clearer goal for you to aim for with your child than 'coping with friends on her own'. Specific aims like that are easier to achieve than are vague ideas.
- *tell your child what each aim is:* let your child know what it is you hope she will achieve. That way you both have a clear idea of what has to be done. It also means that with certain

tasks, such as putting on her socks, she can practise when you are not with her.

- *improve independence in gradual stages:* slow and small steps towards independence are easier to achieve than huge jumps. When trying to teach your child to drink out of a cup on her own without spilling the drink make the first stage that she should lift the cup to her mouth even if she does not drink from it. Then aim for her to touch the cup to her lips. Then aim for one or two drops to go into her mouth, and so on. The desired skill will be achieved eventually if it is broken down into small steps.
- *love and praise:* independence training can be stressful for the child, especially when she experiences failure along the way. Give her lots of praise when she does become more competent at each task and reassure her that she will be able to do it eventually. Your encouragement is crucial.
- *have realistic expectations of your child:* you may feel social pressures to push your child to achieve at a level more advanced than normally expected of a child that age. But remember that all children are different.
- *don't rush your child:* give her plenty of time to achieve the specific task. A child desperately trying to dress herself in the morning can be highly inconvenient for the rest of the family who want to get out of the house in time for school or work. You will be tempted to dress her, for the sake of speed, but that only works against independence. Make sure you leave the child enough time to complete the task. The conditions need to be relaxed and supportive, not hurried.
- *explain to the child what you are trying to achieve:* your child might see no advantage in being able to do things for herself and may be content with the status quo. Explain to her why she should be independent, for instance, because she will be able to do something without having to wait for someone else to help her, or because she can make her own choices.

Toilet-training

Control of bowel and bladder is one of a child's major achievements on the road to independence. Parents vary in their attitudes to this. Some believe that toilet-training should be started as soon as possible because of all the inconvenience and expense of nappies, while others believe their child will learn by herself when she is ready. The optimum age to begin toilet-training is between eighteen and twenty-one months, although many parents start a few months earlier or later. There is a wide range in the rate that children learn bladder and bowel control. In many instances, the older the child is before toilet-training begins, then the quicker the success – a two-year-old may learn in a matter of weeks, while a fifteen-month-old infant could take months before she is consistently dry.

Of course, there are cases of parents who claim their baby is potty-trained at six months. By that they mean that when they sit their baby on the potty – and if they leave her on it long enough – she eventually empties her bladder or bowels or both. But that is not bladder and bowel control. Rather it is simply a case of an involuntary reflex muscular movement which happens to take place while the infant is sitting down. Children who 'learn' control at this age very quickly 'unlearn' control as soon as they can get off the potty by themselves, and the whole process of toilet-training has to begin again at a later age.

Toilet-training should begin only when a child shows readiness, which is signified by her awareness that she is passing urine or having a bowel motion. The child indicates this awareness by telling her parents either that her nappy is wet, or when she is actually wetting her nappy, or that she is about to wet her nappy. Where the child does not indicate any such awareness, another sign that she is ready to begin toilet-training is when her nappy is dry even though it has been worn for several hours. Most children learn bladder control after bowel control.

The guidelines given earlier in this chapter for encouraging independence also apply to toilet-training, but the following additional guidelines are specific to toilet-training.

Understanding Children

- *before you even begin training, let your child play with a potty and let her sit on it with her nappy on.* This way she becomes used to the sight of the potty and its name. After this initial phase, gradually explain to her what the potty is for, and keep it beside the toilet bowl.
- *let her go the toilet with her brothers and sisters, or with you – as long as neither you nor they are embarrassed by the presence of a curious toddler.* The child will want to be able to do what the others in her family can do, so the opportunity to watch her older brothers and sisters in the toilet will encourage her to imitate them.
- *once the child is showing signs that she is ready for toilet-training, pick times during the day when you sit her on the potty.* Tell her what you want her to achieve, all the time emphasizing that this is what big children do. Explain to her that you will take her nappy off for a few minutes each time so that she can use the potty. Since you want the child to achieve success wherever possible, make sure the times you select for training are times which you think she usually wets or soils her nappy. The best times are usually after mealtimes or snacktimes.
- *be calm*. Your child may think it is all a big joke, and she may decide to get up and wander about the room after a few moments. As luck will have it, you can be sure that a couple of seconds after she moves away from the potty she will empty her bladder all over the carpet. Try to keep your temper during these occasions. Remind her that she should use the potty and that you will try again later in the day. In the early stages of training, your child is unlikely to ask for the potty consistently. You have to give her regular and frequent opportunities to toilet herself so that she can establish some form of routine with using the potty.
- *allow your child to sit on the potty whether she is toileting or not.* There is no harm in letting your child look at a book while on the potty, or listen to music. If these measures help her feel at ease, then all to the good.
- *don't physically force your child to sit on the potty if she is reluctant.* You are bigger than she so you will have the

Independence

required strength to keep her there. But you cannot force her to empty her bladder or bowels on command. Pressurize her like that and the chances are she will dirty the floor the instant she leaves contact with the potty. Toilet-training has to be done by negotiation and persuasion, not bullying.

- *when your child uses the potty properly – whether by intention or by good fortune – give her lots of praise, and reward her in whatever way you feel is appropriate.* Tell her why you are so pleased, and that soon she may not have to wear a nappy at all.
- *keep the potty handy, within easy reach of the child, so that she can get to it as soon as she feels the need.* Many parents in training their child let her move about the house without a nappy during the day. This is effective as long as she has instant access to the potty.

Toilet-training can be an incredible source of frustration for parents. When it comes to the point that you feel you are engaged in battle with your child, then step back and have a look at what is going on. Freud argued that toilet-training has very profound psychological consequences. He claimed that long-term personality problems could arise from distressing toilet-training experiences. While that rather extreme view is not widely held among psychologists today, most would agree that toilet-training should be as free from tension as possible. True, your child must realize that toilet-training is not a game, that it is an important skill to achieve. But it should not become an area of constant conflict between you and your child.

Keep things in perspective. Don't expect toilet-training to go smoothly, and be prepared for your carpet to get wet and dirty. The calmer you are, and the more routine your manner is when putting your child on the potty, then the quicker she will achieve success. Never punish your child simply because she does not fill the potty at the most convenient moment for you. That will reduce her self-confidence, increase the tension between you, and decrease the speed of her learning.

Children become dry at night after they become dry during

the day, usually between the ages of two and three. This is another stage of independence that the child should be encouraged to achieve. By this time your child is older and more mature. She will probably feel quite confident going to the toilet during the day, and may even prefer using a small toilet seat fitted on to the normal seat instead of the potty. Being toilet-trained during the day, she knows what is required of her at night. The most common sign of readiness for night training is when you find that her night nappy is regularly dry in the morning when she wakes up. Boys frequently take longer than girls to become dry at night. Common-sense rules apply to night training. Make sure the child visits the toilet before going to sleep, check that she can reach the toilet at night if she wakes up (leave a light on in the toilet all night if necessary) or keep the potty close to her bed if that is more convenient; do not give her lots of drinks before she goes to sleep. There is no scientific evidence that a child who wets at night is a very deep sleeper. Research confirms that a child can pass urine at any stage in her sleep, not always at the deepest moment, and most commonly when she is moving from a phase of deep sleep into lighter sleep.

If your child takes months to become dry at night, don't worry: she will achieve it eventually. Give her lots of encouragement, lots of praise when the bed is dry in the morning, and be prepared to wash lots of sheets while she learns. Some parents lift their sleeping child when they themselves are going to bed and take her to the toilet. There is no evidence that this actually works. In fact, this can be counter-productive because it means the parents are taking the responsibility of toilet-training away from their child to themselves. Nor is there any evidence that depriving a child of drinks in the evening will help her become dry at night. Of course, the child should not be plied with glasses of juice prior to bedtime, but even total deprivation will not stop her bladder filling during the night – and it could be a source of conflict between you and your child. By all means, take these measures if they make you feel more in control of toilet-training, but don't expect them to teach the child bladder control at night.

Independence

The child of three or four who starts to wet at night after she has been dry consistently for a long period may be suffering from an infection or other illness, and this possibility should be investigated by the family doctor, but it is more likely that the wetting is due to an emotional difficulty. Many first-born children, who are dry during the day and night, begin to be wet at night when a younger brother or sister is born. The stress of having another child in the family causes the first-born child to lose bladder control temporarily. Other children lose their bladder control when they start playgroup or nursery. But these phases are usually temporary and bladder control returns when the child feels less harassed. Seek advice from your health visitor or doctor if the problem persists.

Constipation is a common physical cause of soiling. In this condition the bowel becomes packed with solid waste matter and the fluid in the bowel starts to leak out, causing soiling. Medical treatment for constipation is straightforward and works quickly. However, many instances of soiling are linked to emotional difficulties, often arising from a child's reaction against an over-rigorous and over-orderly regime in the household. Psychologists claim that a parent who is very concerned about neatness, who deals very rigidly with a child and who allows that child very little opportunity to show independence, may find she reacts against this unconsciously by soiling herself. Soiling is the child's way of 'getting back at' her parents – a way that is extremely distressing for everyone concerned. Change will occur when the parents become more flexible in managing their child. Psychological help may be necessary if the soiling becomes an established pattern.

Untying the apron strings

The road to independence in childhood stretches outside the house. What you do to encourage your child to be independent at home is very important, but how your child copes with social situations when you are not there is also an important part of independence. Many parents start to get their child used to short separations, even when a baby, by encouraging her to

Understanding Children

spend a few moments in the arms of someone else, by leaving her in the care of a friend or relative for a few minutes, or by having her sleep in a separate room as soon as she comes home from the maternity hospital. When she is older her parents might deliberately encourage her to spend a few hours at a friend's house, or they might leave her in the care of a child minder. Early experience of short separations from parents – separations not due to ill-health or trauma – can be part of independence training and help lay the foundations for later self-sufficiency.

The first major separation from you in the young child's life is the start at playgroup or nursery. Perhaps for the first time your child is away from you, having to stand on her own without you holding her hand. A distressful reaction to the start at playgroup or nursery is commonplace, but you can take positive steps to help your child through this phase:

- *prepare your child for the event by talking about it to her beforehand*. Do this well before she is due to start there, and visit the playgroup or nursery before the start of term to familiarize her with the adults there and the building.
- *be calm and relaxed when taking the child there each day*. You will probably feel anxious, particularly on the first day, because the start at nursery is the end of one chapter in her life. But do not show any sign of your concern. If you child does appear to be worried, reassure her that there is nothing for her to be concerned about.
- *do not linger at the playgroup or nursery once you have arrived there*. Leave promptly, even if she appears upset. Furthermore, hand the child over to one of the staff so that she has someone to look after her.
- *talk about the day's events when you collect her at the end of the session*. That will encourage her interest in the nursery activities.

The child who is reluctant to separate from her parents needs their help. And the best help they can give her is to be caring, sensitive ... but resolute. The child has to be absolutely

Independence

certain that the separation will take place whether she wants it or not, and that her tears will not change anything. Be determined to see your plan of action through. Your child will accept what you are asking of her, once she realizes that you mean what you say. And you will find she is a stronger and more mature individual with her new-found level of independence. When the child attends the 'big school' at the age of five, the experience of coping with playgroup or nursery gives her that extra confidence.

Reluctance to start playgroup or nursery usually passes within a few weeks. But if complaints from the child continue, or if she starts to say she feels ill whenever nursery is mentioned, then the problem may be deeper than a passing childhood phase. In that situation the parents should look further into the child's life. Her anxiety might stem from something going on inside the nursery, such as bullying from other children, or uncaring handling from staff members. Or it might stem from something outside the nursery, such as low self-confidence, or fear of being rejected by her parents. Whatever the reason for the child's anxiety, the parents have to investigate the possible causes until they have identified what is troubling the child, and have taken corrective action.

Chapter 14

Self-Image

Psychologists attribute great importance to 'self-image' because of its impact on personality development. The terms 'self-image', 'self-concept' or 'self-esteem' (all of which refer to the same idea) are defined as a child's sense of being a unique individual, the feelings of personal worth he has, and the way he sees himself in relation to other children and adults. A good self-image is an essential ingredient of personal happiness and contentment with oneself. Many individuals requiring psychological help have a poor self-concept and strong feelings of personal inadequacy.

Research studies indicate that children with a poor self-image:

- find difficulty in giving love to or receiving love from other children and adults including their parents.
- do not relate well to their peers and feel socially isolated from those around them.
- tend to make derogatory remarks about anything they do even when these achievements are of a satisfactory standard.
- are more likely to be ashamed of themselves, to have guilt feelings and even to be depressed.
- have a higher level of anxiety and therefore find everyday experiences unusually stressful.
- have difficulty in being honest in their relationships with other people because of a lack of trust in themselves.
- are defensive when relating to other children and adults and assume the worst of everyone.

- take longer to settle down when they start primary school, and have slower academic progress.

Components of the self-concept

A child's self-image has four main components. First, there is the 'looking-glass self' – the ideas he has about himself that are derived from the way other people react towards him. The child who is constantly told that he is stupid will have doubts about his ability and may not try hard at school. The boy who is constantly reminded that he is not well co-ordinated may be afraid to embark on sporting activities. And the child who is told by his friends that they want to play football with him because he is skilful, will be enthusiastic when playing. A child's social relationships, therefore, help to shape his self-concept.

Second, self-image is affected by the extent to which a child compares himself to other children his own age. This type of self-comparison is a natural part of development, allowing a child to judge the strength of his own qualities and skills in relation to those children he knows. That helps the child evaluate himself. Yet, the effect of such comparisons can extend well into adulthood. One study found that girls who are much taller than other girls at the age of thirteen continue to regard themselves as taller throughout their adult life, even when any previous height difference no longer exists.

Third, everybody has different roles in life. You will play a wide range of roles, such as the role of parent, of partner, of colleague, of best friend, and so on. Each role makes different demands on you, requiring you to act in different ways and affecting the way you see yourself. In each role you learn new information about yourself and your capabilities. Sometimes this information is positive (when, in the role of manager, you learn that you are capable of resolving complex problems at work). Sometimes the information is negative (when, in the role of parent, you learn that you are unable to control your two-year-old's behaviour). All this information is integrated into your self-concept. A young child is no different from you in this respect. It is true that his roles – such as child, friend, and pupil – are less complex than most adult roles, but they have equal impact on the way he sees himself.

The last major component of a child's self-concept derives from the process of identification. Every child identifies with people in his life, usually his mother and father, but he can also identify with his friends and other adults that he knows. Through this, a child begins to adopt the ideas and behaviour of the person with whom he is identifying, and this in turn influences the feelings of personal worth the child has for himself.

Parents

Through the four components of self-image, parents exert the most significant influence on their child's self-concept. Children who have a strong self-image tend to have parents who:

- have a strong self-image themselves
- are psychologically stable and settled
- are able to cope with life
- appear to be calm under pressure
- have clear ideas on the way children should be brought up.

Parent–child interactions have also been found to be crucial. In contrast to mothers of children with a poor self-image, mothers of children with a strong self-concept are usually more accepting of the child's strengths and weaknesses. The mother and her child are able to communicate easily and can convey loving emotions easily to each other. This type of mother is interested in her child's day-to-day experiences and makes an effort to help her child achieve in any task he is attempting. On the other hand, where a mother is less attentive to her child's emotional needs and is disinterested in what he does, that child is more likely to have a poor self-image. Parents who are derogatory about their child, or even indifferent about their relationships with him, will not encourage him to feel positively about himself.

Family discipline

Your child's self-concept is affected by the way you maintain rules within your family home. Children with high self-esteem tend to have parents who:

- are likely to enforce rules in the home consistently
- prefer to use rewards to encourage the desired behaviour rather than punishments to discourage rule-breaking
- even when they punish their child, do so in a manner that is straightforward and appropriate in intensity to the actual misdemeanour
- make an effort to explain to the child why the punishment is being given
- consider the child's point of view when setting rules so that the child feels his opinion matters.

On the other hand, children with low self-esteem tend to have parents who:

- do not offer their child much guidance on how to behave, due more to their indifference than to actual detailed planning
- let the child's misbehaviour go on for a long time until they can tolerate it no longer, often grossly over-reacting when they finally do discipline their child
- tend to use excessive punishment when chastising their child for misbehaviour
- use punishment to enforce rules in preference to using positive incentives to induce acceptable behaviour from their child
- use physical punishment.

Improving your child's self-concept

You can help your child improve his self-concept. The following suggestions will give you some direction:

- *take an interest in all that your child does, in the minor as well as the major aspects of his day-to-day life;* let your child see that you

care about what he is doing, and that you want to hear about his experiences.
- *emphasize your child's strong points, especially when he feels he is not as capable as other children;* whenever he makes comparisons of himself against his friends, always encourage him to make these comparisons as broad as possible so that he does not focus on only one aspect.
- *even when your child misbehaves, don't repeatedly tell him how bad he is;* constant reminders of his negative aspects will reduce his self-respect; always try to find some positive aspects of his behaviour and achievements that you can praise.
- *take your child's wishes and feelings into account when making decisions about what he is allowed to do;* let him make choices about minor events in his life, such as what biscuits he eats, what juice he drinks, and so on.
- *provide experiences in which your child is likely to be successful and avoid experiences in which you know he is bound to fail;* the best boost to a child's self-image is success.
- *have realistic expectations of your child's abilities and achievements;* avoid placing your child in situations that you think are likely to prove too demanding for him.

Disability and self-image

Since self-image is affected by the reaction of others, the child with a physical disability faces particular problems when he interacts with people outside his immediate family. Throughout his early development, his parents will have spent a great deal of time encouraging him to cope using the skills he has. A child who has limited movement in his legs will have been shown how to move around the house using a rollator (a support frame on castors), a wheelchair, or whatever. A child who has a cleft palate and unclear speech will have been shown how to make his voice as clear as possible. And a child who has a facial deformity may in fact have stopped noticing it because nobody in the family draws attention to it. Within the home, the child with a physical disability or physical deformity will probably have a good self-image and be full of self-confidence.

Self-Image

Stepping outside the confines of the family environment, the child is likely to come into contact with other children and adults who are not as supportive as his parents are. He will meet people who stare at him, people who go out of their way to avoid him because they feel uncomfortable in his presence, and people who ask him questions about his disability or deformity. These reactions can have an adverse effect on the child, reducing his confidence and lowering his self-esteem. Therefore, parents should discuss some possible reactions of others with their child before he attends nursery or school. They should explain that other children might not understand the effects of his disability and that as a result they may say things that will upset him. But at the same time, the parents should emphasize his strengths: for instance, that he has a pleasing personality, that he is co-operative, or that he is bright and inquisitive. A small amount of preparation before the child ventures into the outside world can help prevent his self-image from taking a tumble.

The 'looking-glass self' can work positively for children. Down's Syndrome – a congenital form of delayed development – causes very distinct facial features, such as slanting eyes, low nose bridge, small mouth and protruding tongue. These characteristics make Down's Syndrome children immediately identifiable and adults who associate the condition with limited development will instantly have lower expectations of such a child. However, controversial medical research has used reconstructive facial surgery to make Down's Syndrome children look less distinctive, more like the general population, in the hope that this might result in an all-round improvement in their development. Results have been encouraging – the children who have undergone this surgery function better and more independently in society. One explanation is that because a Down's Syndrome child after cosmetic surgery looks more 'normal' other children and adults interact more normally with him. The child's self-image is enhanced as a result of this new social reaction towards him, and consequently he is more able to cope with the demands of his environment.

Understanding Children

A sense of gender

Gender identity (that is, the sense of 'boyness' and 'girlness') is a crucial component of a child's self-concept. Watch a group of young children playing and you will see each of them identifying with different characters. Boys play boys' games and girls play girls' games. But psychologists claim that difference does not happen simply because of anatomical differences between boys and girls. The attitudes of a child's parents, in particular, and the attitude of society, in general, play a large part in the development of gender identity.

Development of gender identity starts from birth, with the very language that adults use towards their babies. You will not find many fathers describing their baby boy as 'pretty', nor will you find many mothers describing their baby girl as 'well built'. We use one set of words for boys and another for girls as soon as they are born. And already the foundations for a separate gender identity are laid.

Sex differentiation also shows through in clothes and toys preferences. The very first outfit bought for the newborn baby will either be pink (for a girl) or blue (for a boy). Few adults would be bold enough to challenge this social convention by purchasing a pair of blue bootees for their baby daughter. Nor would they consider buying a doll for their baby son. This separation of the sexes through clothes and toys continues from then on, right through childhood. There is nothing inherently wrong, for example, for a boy to wear a skirt – in fact in some societies they do. But society lays down clear rules about who should wear what clothes, and this affects the way parents dress their children.

Your child's gender identity is well formed by school age, and he will already have a very fixed idea of what qualities a male has and what qualities a female has. Most children of that age consider that:

- males have more physical strength than females
- boys fight more than girls
- girls get hurt more easily than boys

Self-Image

- boys and girls wear different clothes
- boys are not expected to show emotion as openly as girls
- girls are expected to be more helpless when under stress.

Differentiation of boys and girls by their parents manifests itself in other ways in the pre-school years. Mothers behave differently towards boys. Research confirms that mothers tend to keep a baby girl closer to them and spend more time in direct contact with her than they do with a baby boy. Mothers encourage boys to be independent more than they encourage girls. Parents criticize and praise girls more than boys, and fathers are more concerned than mothers that their child plays in stereotyped ways.

Children's books often present boys and girls in a very stereotyped way, endorsing the ideas on gender promoted by society. And usually it is the boy's role that appears more interesting and more highly valued. In recent years, parents and educationists have become increasingly concerned about this aspect of children's literature. Now there are many stereotype-free books available in local libraries. These texts present the story without the children in them adopting traditional sex roles. You have to decide for yourself what you think is the right reading material for your child, but at least now there is a wider choice.

This process of sex differentiation affects a child's achievements throughout childhood. Sex differences have a very real impact on children as they grow up. Research findings indicate that:

- girls tend to develop language at an earlier age and at a faster rate than boys
- in speech girls tend to use longer sentences and have greater fluency
- advantages in language acquisition carry into the primary school, where girls frequently learn to read faster than boys
- remedial difficulties in reading and spelling are four times more common in boys than girls
- pre-school girls are happy to play with boys their own age but boys of that age are rarely happy to play with girls

- young boys prefer physical rough-and-tumble games while girls enjoy more sedate, organized activities
- in disagreements with children their own age, boys are more likely than girls to resort to physical violence
- girls prefer to conform to the standards of behaviour that are expected of them, whereas boys are not so concerned at fitting in.

Examination results consistently show that boys have higher achievements than girls in maths and science. Some psychologists claim that this is because boys are biologically predisposed to learning maths and science, that there are genetic reasons for male mathematical superiority. Others claim that this is because boys are positively encouraged to achieve in these academic areas while girls are not. This view is given support by the fact that school timetables often make maths and science compulsory subjects for boys but optional for girls. In addition girls in single-sex schools tend to score more in maths and science exams than girls in co-educational schools, suggesting that teacher expectations play a part. Universities now take this division between the sexes seriously and many science and engineering departments have open days solely for girls in the hope of stimulating their interest in these subjects.

You may be content for your child to adopt a traditional sex role, or you may feel that you would like your child to absorb the best from both sets of gender expectations. It is a matter of personal choice. Bear in mind, though, that some individuals are more comfortable in untypical roles. For instance, the top cooks and fashion designers – skills most frequently associated with women – are mostly men. Crossing the boundaries is possible though there is no value in doing this for its own sake. Yet there could be benefits if such action helps children achieve their full potential.

The self-fulfilling prophecy

R. K. Merton – a psychologist concerned with the way people are influenced by their own expectations – took the notion of

Self-Image

the self-concept being subject to social influences one stage further. He put forward the idea of the self-fulfilling prophecy – the idea that if a person has specific expectations of us then we shall behave in ways to confirm that expectation. In other words, the self-fulfilling prophecy becomes true simply because it has been made.

A startling demonstration of this was given by a group of researchers who looked into the effects of teachers' expectations on pupil progress. These researchers looked at 650 pupils between the ages of five and ten. The pupils' teachers were told that the children had all been assessed intellectually and that they had been divided into three groups. The first group of children were expected to achieve the most educationally, the second group of children were expected to have average attainments and the third group were expected to make minimal progress during the school. The teachers were told which pupils in their class fell into each group. In fact, the researchers had randomly allocated the children to each group, although the teachers did not know that. By measuring the pupils' progress at the end of the school year, the researchers would be able to determine the effect, if any, of the self-fulfilling prophecy. Under normal conditions all three groups would make similar progress.

The results showed that the first group (identified to the teachers as the top group) had the highest achievements of all, the second group (identified as the average group) had lower achievements educationally, and the third group (identified as the poorest group) made the smallest amount of educational progress. Therefore, there is some substance to the self-fulfilling prophecy and it can have an effect on child development. Clearly it does not mean that if you have certain expectations of your child then he will always meet them. Raising children is not as easy as that. But it does suggest that higher expectations of your child are more likely to lead to his success than having lower expectations.

Chapter 15

Language Development

Spoken language is a child's main means of communication. Bear in mind, though, that long before the young child is able to talk, she is able to communicate her feelings non-verbally. A newborn baby conveys her distress by crying – her parents know straightaway what that means even though she is not using words. At around six weeks, many babies are able to use a smile to indicate their pleasure. The baby who has had enough to eat gets this message across to her parents easily by spitting out her food, or by pushing the teat out of her mouth using her tongue.

Not all communication between parents and babies is as basic as this. Sophisticated camera techniques have enabled psychologists to film the interaction between a mother and her young baby. By slowing down the film many times, researchers were able to see a lot more communication going on between a mother and her baby than appeared at first sight. They confirmed that a baby is capable of 'pre-speech' – a very basic form of turn-taking in conversation – when an adult speaks to it. The slowed-down film revealed that when a mother talks to her young baby, amid its seemingly unco-ordinated babbling, a complex interaction is taking place. The baby appears to fit its vocalizations into the gaps between its mother's sentences, almost as if it is listening to what is being said and then replying. Psychologists regard this as the very earliest sign of a baby's capacity for language.

As a child matures from babyhood into infancy, her desire

to use language becomes more evident. She begins to make sounds that have some similarity to word syllables, even though she cannot speak in actual words. Toddlers can become very frustrated when they cannot make themselves understood. Psychologists claim this frustration underlies many of the tantrums displayed by pre-verbal infants. Parents often find their previously frustrated child becomes more settled once she can communicate using language rather than gestures.

How children learn language

If you have ever tried to learn a second language yourself, as an adult, you will realize what a complex task this is. Imagine if the language you had to learn was English. There are thousands of words to be remembered, endless grammatical rules, and a long list of words with more than one meaning. Then there are words that sound the same but have different spelling patterns (*their/there*), and words that have similar spelling patterns but sound different (*cough/bough*). You would probably think it was an impossible task to master. Yet virtually all children learn a full language system before they reach the age of five. It is almost as if babies have been pre-programmed to learn language in a certain way, as if they are born with an innate ability to develop a meaningful language system.

This idea of an innate language ability is one theory psychologists use to explain how children learn language. This theory proposes that a baby is genetically endowed with a 'Language Acquisition Device' – an inborn device that predisposes the developing child to recognize certain types of word and grammatical structure when she hears them. The language acquisition device enables the child to pick out the important parts of the speech that she hears. The problem with this theory is that it suggests that the child's environment is unimportant since she will learn language in whatever context she is raised. But a child's language is greatly influenced by her family upbringing.

Understanding Children

An alternative theory of language development comes from behaviourist psychologists who maintain that a child has no inborn notion of language whatsoever. Instead, the behaviourist argues that a child learns certain words and word structures because her parents reward her when she uses them. When the child points to a glass of juice and says the word 'juice', her parents smile, lavish her with praise for having used the word in its proper context, and then reward her even further by giving her the juice. That type of interaction, says the behaviourist, occurs many times every day and that is how a child learns to speak. The difficulty with this theory, however, is that it cannot explain why a child picks out only certain words of the thousands she hears each day. And then there is the difficulty in explaining how a child can invent new words – for instance, the two-year-old who says 'milk gone-ded' – even though she has never been taught this by her parents in the past.

There seems to be an element of truth in both these theories, though neither is sufficient on its own. Language learning is probably a combination of inborn language skills and the effect of the child's environment. Either way, there are certain strategies you should adopt for encouraging your child's use of language.

- *talk to your baby;* you may feel foolish talking to a week-old baby who appears to have no idea what you are saying, but, even in these very early stages, parental speech is an important stimulus for the baby. It allows the baby to see language has a purpose, it stimulates her interest, and develops her listening skills. You will find as the baby grows older that she begins to imitate your sounds.
- *respond to any sounds she makes;* a baby has a wide variety of sounds that she uses when babbling. Sometimes these sounds are just for her own pleasure, especially when she is playing alone in her cot, but most times they are used to attract your attention. The more you respond to her vocalizations then the more likely she is to continue making them.
- *read story books to her;* even a young infant, who has no

formal speech of her own, will enjoy having stories read to her. This stimulates her interest in language, and also in books. The closeness of parent and baby during story-time is another incentive to language development.
- *let your child listen to songs, music and poems;* these will provide her with another source of amusement and at the same time she is likely to attempt to sing along. Filling in the last word of a nursery rhyme is also a popular game for the young child who is beginning to speak.
- *talk to her in your usual voice;* there is no need to modify your words to include 'baby-talk'. The child has as much chance of understanding what 'dog' means as she has of understanding what 'bow-wow' means. All that baby-talk teaches a child is a language which she will have to modify as soon as she is a little older. Talk to your child using your normal voice. She will pick out the important words from your speech.
- *give your child a chance to speak;* it is all too easy in families to relegate the children's language to second place. At the end of a difficult day, you have lots of information to exchange with your partner. But your child also needs to be given an opportunity to speak as well. Let her tell you her news, however trivial that might be when compared to your own experiences that day. And ask her questions about what she tells you. Even the child who only has a few words of speech will thrive under that form of parental attention.
- *avoid constantly correcting your child when she makes a mistake in her speech;* learning language takes time and it is only natural that a child should have some difficulties along the way. Continual correction of errors will reduce the child's confidence and make her reluctant to talk at all.

Slow language development

Although children vary in the rate at which they acquire speech, there are specific 'milestones' of speech development which are common to all children at approximately the same age. (These development stages are discussed in the Development

Checklists at the end of this book.) Most parents are aware when their child is slow to learn to speak, because they compare her to other children the same age, or to their previous children. If you are concerned about possible slow language development then you should seek professional advice through your GP, who will refer the child to a psychologist or a speech therapist, depending on the nature of the child's difficulty.

Minor speech difficulties

A child may have a speech difficulty, even though all other areas of her development are satisfactory. In such cases, the speech difficulty is the child's sole problem and either clears up spontaneously, or else responds to help from a speech therapist. These difficulties include:

- *lisping:* children often develop a lisp in the pre-school years. Many begin to make letter substitutes, such as 'th' for 's', 'f' for 'th', and so on. Fortunately, these speech patterns pass as the child matures, usually by the time she reaches school. A child might acquire a temporary lisp when her first teeth begin to fall out, but again this lasts only for a short while until her second teeth grow in. A lisp can also be caused by misuse of the tongue, or by a cleft palate. Speech therapy is helpful in these instances.
- *mispronunciations:* learning to speak takes time, and making mistakes is part of the learning process. Many children experience difficulty with certain sounds. This results in the child's speech being unclear. Again, this defect usually disappears spontaneously as a child becomes more mature and more experienced linguistically. If a child's speech is still unclear by the time she is nearing school age, then speech therapy may be required.
- *lack of stimulation:* speech development partly depends on a child's interaction with others in her family. By listening to everyone in her family talking to her, the infant's interest in language is stimulated. She needs that type of individual

attention to spur on her language acquisition. However, in certain circumstances this may not be readily available. The youngest child in a large family, a child who has a brother or sister close in age, or a child who is cared for by someone who speaks very little themselves, may suffer from lack of stimulation. Once this is identified as being the cause, the remedy is simple – lots of individual attention using discussions, stories, song and poems.

- *stammering (also called stuttering):* with this defect, a child talks very hesitantly, perhaps repeating the first letter or first part of a word several times. It is almost as though the child is trying to sort out her thoughts while she stutters. Many children between the ages of two and five develop some form of stutter, probably because there is so much they want to say all at once. This temporary form of speech impediment clears up as the child becomes more confident in her use of language. The cardinal rules when interacting with a stuttering child are never make fun of her, never imitate her, and never become impatient with her. If you do, her stutter will simply become more extreme. Speech therapy techniques are able to help stutterers gain more control over their speech.

Language delay as an indicator of developmental delay

Slowness to develop language can be a sign of a general developmental delay. This type of child will also be slow in learning to sit up on her own, in learning to walk, in learning bladder control, in becoming independent, and in learning to socialize with other children. The earlier this type of difficulty is detected then the sooner the child will be able to receive help to stimulate her development. Parents concerned about their child's development should discuss this with their GP or health visitor. If these professionals are in doubt at all about the nature of the child's speech delay, they will arrange for specialist developmental assessment by a child psychologist.

Hearing difficulties

Hearing loss, whether total or partial, is the single most common reason underlying a child's failure to develop normal speech. Estimates suggest that approximately one child in ten has a mild hearing loss, and that approximately one child in a thousand has a severe hearing loss or total deafness. The hearing-impaired baby has a number of difficulties. First, she cannot hear the everyday sounds which stimulate the baby with normal hearing. Second, she gets no feedback from her own speech because she can't hear the sounds she is making. A deaf baby starts to make sounds at around the same age as a hearing baby, but the lack of feedback means she has less encouragement to practise and enlarge her range of vocalizations. And third, she can't hear what is being said to her by other children and adults. Hearing difficulties impair the child's abilities to interact with other people, and can cause a sense of isolation.

Babbling and listening to sounds provide the foundation for later speech development. The child who misses out these early experiences as a baby will find that learning to speak is harder than it is for the child with normal hearing. The hearing-impaired child may be slower to speak, she may not use her first words until long after the age she is expected to, and she may be slower to understand the meaning of words. The sooner a hearing loss is identified then the sooner action can be taken to help the child – the longer a child's hearing loss goes undetected, then the greater will be the delay in her language learning.

Signs of hearing loss

Hearing loss is difficult to detect because the baby cannot indicate her difficulty. As far as the partially hearing baby is concerned, hearing muffled sounds is normal. Therefore, parents have to look for behavioural signs that something is wrong. If you are concerned that your baby might not be hearing properly, ask yourself the following questions:

Language Development

- *does she respond to your voice?* The baby should show an almost immediate reaction when you speak to her, either by turning her head towards you or else by at least showing some change in her behaviour at the time. Failure, or slowness, to react could be important.
- *does your baby seem to be soothed by your voice if you are not in her line of vision?* Most babies when distressed will be soothed by their mother's comforting voice and will become calmer. However, the hearing-impaired baby may only be soothed when she can actually see her mother.
- *is your baby startled when someone comes into her line of vision?* Babies with normal hearing are soon able to anticipate the arrival of another person by the sounds they make. Footsteps coming closer, or the noise of the bedroom door opening, are sounds the hearing baby uses to judge that someone is coming up to them. The hearing-disabled child has no such anticipatory cues and hence may be alarmed when somebody suddenly appears in her line of vision.
- *do your baby's sounds continue to progress after the age of six months?* Even up to the age of six months, a hearing-impaired baby will make the normal range of sounds despite the fact she cannot hear them herself. But whereas a hearing baby's sounds continue to increase and become more elaborate after that age, a deaf baby's speech does not and she may even use her voice less.
- *can your baby locate a sound source?* By the age of two months, a baby with normal hearing will react to a sound by turning her eyes or head towards it. Try talking to the baby or shaking a rattle when she is not looking at you – but do it gently or you may frighten her. The partially hearing or deaf baby will not respond or else may seem confused because she can't tell where the sound is coming from.
- *does your baby always turn the same ear towards a sound source, irrespective of the direction of the noise?* A baby with normal hearing will turn the left or right side of her head towards a sound, depending on the direction it is coming from. The baby who always turns the same ear towards the sound source may have a hearing loss in one ear only.

Understanding Children

As your baby becomes older, detection of hearing loss becomes easier. The hearing child aged three and upwards will interact happily with her friends and family, whereas the partially hearing or deaf child will not have such a well-developed system of communication. Some of the following indicators of hearing loss could also be due to the child's egocentricity or disobedience, but you should still look out for them:

- *does your child respond quickly and accurately to a simple request?* The young child should be able to react quickly to a basic command. Of course, your child may be pretending not to hear you, but if this happens consistently there may be a hearing difficulty.
- *does your child not stop when she is told to and come to you when asked?* Again, this behaviour may be a sign of your child's unwillingness to co-operate with you. Yet repeated instances of this behaviour may be a sign of a partial-hearing loss.
- *do you find that you have to repeat questions all the time to your child before she responds?* The child with normal hearing should be able to interpret questions that are put to her, without them having to be repeated. The partially hearing child can be very confused in question-and-answer situations.
- *does your child watch your face and mouth very closely during a conversation with her?* The child with hearing loss needs other cues to understand what you are saying, apart from the actual words you are using. She may rely on lip reading and other facial cues to make sense of what she is hearing.
- *is your child's speech development delayed?* Not every speech defect is caused by hearing difficulties, although many are. There are several vocal characteristics more common in the speech of partially hearing children than in the speech of children with normal hearing; for example, speech will be of low quality with the ends of words missing; the range of the child's vocabulary will be restricted in comparison to other children her age; she may mix up letters in her speech, such as 't' and 'k', or 'd' and 'g'; there may be no detectable

difference in her words between the 'sh' and 's' sounds.
- *does she have a high level of frustration?* The child with partial, or total, hearing loss usually becomes easily frustrated because she can't understand what is going on. Tantrums in a young child are part of normal development, but severe tantrums, in conjunction with some of the other signs, may reflect a hearing difficulty.

None of the above indicators by themselves necessarily mean that the child has a hearing loss, since lack of responsiveness could be due to the child's temperament. However, should you find the above patterns of behaviour are being repeated every day, then discuss it with your GP. A survey on hearing loss showed that in three cases out of four, the difficulty was first suspected by the child's parents whereas only one case in twenty was first suspected by a doctor. And be prepared to persevere. One survey looked at referrals of possible hearing loss to family doctors and found that half of all family doctors consulted by parents of children who were later found to be deaf did not agree the child was deaf. A third of these doctors refused referral to a specialist. Once a child reaches a specialist, far fewer omissions are made.

Encouraging language development in a hearing-impaired child

The diagnosis that a child has a hearing loss can be very distressing. Yet parents have a major role in determining the full effect of their child's hearing difficulty. A child with hearing loss has the right to participate in her family along with her brothers and sisters. She should be allowed the same opportunities for self-development and be allowed to establish her independence and self-confidence. The way you respond to the child at home will greatly influence her ability to cope. All those suggestions for stimulating language development, given earlier in this chapter, also apply to the child with a hearing loss. In addition, the following points will provide you with further ideas:

- *toys:* these help stimulate the child's interest. In the early weeks of life, a baby will be aware of a rattle hanging near her. If hearing loss has been diagnosed at this age choose a rattle that is brightly coloured and one that lets her feel vibrations when it is shaken. At around six months, when the child is able to sit on her own, music often has great appeal. A solid toy music box or portable radio held close to the child will enable her actually to feel beat and rhythm. Towards the end of the first year, games that present different sounds in different places will be useful, for instance, peek-a-boo with all sorts of musical instruments encourages the child to locate noises. Past this age, toy shops are full of games that provide learning, language and listening experiences.
- *hearing aids:* make sure your child wears a hearing aid if it has been prescribed by the ear, nose and throat consultant. Hearing aids can make sounds louder for the listener, though a deaf child will still not hear words exactly as a child with normal hearing does. Your child might not be comfortable wearing the aid, and may feel embarrassed by it, but the aid should be worn continually at the correct adjustment. Modern hearing aids are extremely powerful and can offer substantial help to a child with hearing loss.
- *meaningful conversation:* resist the temptation to be stilted and exaggerated when conversing with a hearing-disabled child. Your child must see that speaking has a purpose – and a dull unenthusiastic exchange of words is unlikely to give her that impression. Make a special effort to understand what she has to say. Continued failure to communicate increases the child's frustration and anger.
- *accurate speech:* don't make your child repeat everything she says, but instead say back to the child what she has been trying to communicate to you. For example, if she indicates that she wants a glass of juice, then you should say 'you want a glass of juice?' That way she will be able to hear the proper words and learn from them.
- *mature speech:* some adults talk to a hearing-disabled child at the level of the child's language, not the level of the child's

age or intellect. This means the child hears babyish speech from you. Better not to modify your own speech in this manner. Always speak using your normal language structures.
- *sensitivity:* don't overlook your child's social and emotional development. Deaf children are more prone to behaviour problems than are hearing children because communication is such a struggle for them. Frustrations build up and tantrums are more frequent. But that does not mean a child with hearing loss should be pitied. Treat your hearing-disabled child as you treat your other children – that is the best way to encourage her all-round development.

Chapter 16

Stealing, Lying and Swearing

A newborn baby has no conscience, no sense of right and wrong. As far as a baby is concerned, if he wants something then he should get it. When he is hungry and desires more milk, he cries. It does not matter to the baby whether he has just been fed a few minutes ago, or whether his parents are tired and need a rest before attending to him. A baby thinks only of himself. Issues of morality do not enter into his world.

Moral development gets under way once the infant begins to interact with others, especially his mother and father. He learns that certain behaviour is acceptable while other behaviour is not. At first, the infant may have no idea why he gets into trouble for doing something. But by the age of two or three, a child begins to have some moral sense and is able to make elementary decisions about minor moral issues, for instance, whether he should play with a fragile glass ornament when his parents have warned him not to, but the child's understanding of right and wrong remains limited at that age.

A pre-school child judges the naughtiness of an action in terms of its outcome, not in terms of the underlying intention. Read this story to a pre-school child: *Jane was playing with paints at home. She thought it would be fun to put some paint on the walls. Jane carefully put a small dab of blue paint on one of the walls. Jane's friend, Beth, was also playing with paints at home. By accident, Beth knocked over the paints, and they fell all over the carpet making a terribly big mess.* Then ask the child: *Who was*

Stealing, Lying and Swearing

naughtier, Jane or Beth? A child who is just beginning to develop a sense of morality will regard Beth as the naughtier child because her actions had the more serious consequences, and will judge the morality of his own behaviour in terms of how he is personally affected by the consequences. By the age of five or six, the balance of moral judgements changes. At this age a child begins to appreciate that intentions are part of morality, although he still judges the morality of an action in terms of its implications for him. And the older child of ten or eleven judges the rightness or wrongness of actions in terms of group standards. In particular, the child recognizes family values and has an intrinsic desire to behave in such a way as to attain family approval. For instance, he will not misbehave in a friend's house because he knows that will embarrass his parents.

Parental influences

A child's morality comes from his parents. From birth onwards, the infant begins to identify with his mother and father. Quite simply he wants to be like them. At first, he identifies with them by copying some of their actions. You will be able to recall instances of this with your own child, when he has seen you carrying out a household chore and then imitated your action using his toys. Through this process of identification, a child models his own behaviour on that of his parents.

But identification goes further than that. As well as behaving like his parents, a child begins to think like them. He begins to adopt their attitudes and values, and their moral standards. In the early stages of this, when the child is two or three years old, he still needs his parents to enforce the rules of behaviour. He still needs them to remind him what he can and cannot do. Yet, within a few years, the child will have internalized many of his parents' attitudes to right and wrong. This means that he knows how to behave even when his parents are not with him telling him what to do. Their conscience has become his, and one indication of this is that he experiences guilt when he transgresses.

Understanding Children

Strategies to promote your child's moral awareness – whether you are dealing with lying, stealing, or swearing – include:

- *explain each rule to your child in terms that he can understand.* Simply telling a child what the rules are will not bring about his moral understanding. The child requires an explanation that he can relate to. If your child damages another child's drawing at school, of course you should reprimand him. But at the same time you should explain why his action is wrong, for instance, because he would not like it if his painting was torn or because the other children in the class would think badly of him.
- *put moral rules very clearly and specifically to your child.* There is no point in expecting a young child to be able to apply general ethical principles to specific instances. For instance, instead of saying to the child who has just smashed up his best friend's toy car 'It's not nice to upset people' it would be more effective to say 'Don't break someone else's toys because they will cry and they might break your toys in return.' Start with specific rules and as your child matures he will be able to extend them himself to cover more general situations.
- *react reasonably when your child misbehaves.* The most effective type of punishment is that which is balanced against the seriousness of the crime. You may find it upsetting to discover that your child has scribbled on his newly decorated bedroom wall, but that does not mean he should be banned from having sweets for a month. An over-extreme reaction from parents – often based more on the consequences of the child's actions rather than on the underlying intentions – fails to give a child any sense of perspective on punishment. Your methods of punishing the child have to be on a scale of severity matched to the specific misbehaviour.
- *avoid using physical punishment with the child who breaks moral rules.* Psychological research consistently shows that constantly smacking a child for his wrong-doings does not stop a repetition of that same behaviour in the future. Instead, it

Stealing, Lying and Swearing

simply encourages him to be more secretive, in order to avoid punishment, and it also reduces his feelings of guilt.
- *don't put your child in situations that you know will tempt him.* That only puts him under unnecessary pressure. If you do observe your child about to commit some improper action, step in right away at the beginning before he completes what he intends to do. Research shows that is a much more effective technique than punishing the child after the event.
- *emphasize to your child that although you are annoyed with him for doing wrong, you still love him.* Fear of loss of love can be very real for young children. Therefore, punishment for misdemeanours should be accompanied by the reassurance that the child is still loved. He has to learn that parental punishment and parental love are not mutually exclusive.

Stealing

A child under the age of five will not have a full understanding of the significance of personal possessions. True, a young child can get very agitated when her friend takes one of her favourite dolls without asking, but she cannot generalize this concept to other people's possessions. So the young child is not 'stealing' in the adult sense of the word. The best approach with children of that age is to handle any minor incident of theft firmly, explaining to the child why it is wrong to steal. Encourage the child to imagine what it would be like if the same thing happened to her.

Most school-age children 'try out' theft at some time or another. Stealing might provide a solution to the child's current practical problem, like not having enough money to buy sweets, or not having the toy that all the other children have got. The act of stealing will also have an emotional effect on the child. It makes him feel adventurous and exciting – at least until he is caught, at which point he wishes he had never had the idea in the first place. If you do discover your child has stolen something, nip it in the bud there and then. Treat the matter seriously, explain the morality and the consequences of his behaviour, ensure he is involved in compensating the victim, and punish him reasonably (perhaps by stopping his pocket money for a week). As long as your child knows you most strongly disapprove of his behaviour then he is unlikely to repeat it. But don't over-react. Taking a sweet from a shop without paying is hardly the Great Train Robbery. Keep the matter in perspective. A one-off incident does not mean a regular pattern will be established.

Your own behaviour in front of your child influences his perception of theft. Consider six-year-old Simon. His mother was shocked one day to find that the boy had smuggled a coloured pencil out of his classroom when the teacher was not watching him. She was angry with Simon, and told him how wrong it was to steal things from people, that he should not take someone's possessions without asking them, and that he would have to pay for a replacement out of his pocket money. The boy was very upset. When Simon's father came home from work that evening, his wife intended to tell him about Simon's theft from school. Before she could, the father took two packets of paper clips, a bundle of envelopes and a roll of Sellotape from his pocket, and mentioned that he had managed to take them from the office when no one was looking. Simon looked on confused.

Suppose you found yourself in a similar situation. Would you see any difference between what the child had done and what his father had done? What do you think Simon will learn from this incident? Should the father be punished in the same way as his son? The fact is that double standards of morality confuse children. A child is just as likely to imitate the wrong things that you do as well as the right things. The parental philosophy 'Do as I say, not as I do' does not encourage a child's strong moral development.

Persistent theft by a school-age child is a cause for concern, and may be a sign of a deeper emotional problem. A child who fails to get love and attention from his parents may decide that if he can't get that from them, then at least he is going to get something from them. And so he steals money from his mother's purse, even when he does not want to spend it, or steals biscuits from the food cupboard, even when he is not hungry. Many psychologists claim that this unconscious chain of events frequently underlies incidents of repeated theft. A child in that category still needs to have moral rules explained to him. Yet stealing is only the symptom – it is not the real problem. And the best way parents can tackle that more fundamental dimension of the child's behaviour is to sit down and discuss the child's development with each other. They need to examine the child's life closely, and their relationship with him, to identify possible causes. In severe cases, professional psychological help may be required.

Lying

Lying can be defined as a statement intended to deceive. It is a deliberate attempt to distort the truth and implies an ability to distinguish fact from fantasy. For these reasons, a very young child cannot lie. Under the age of two, an infant may be caught red-handed doing something wrong, and yet will instantly claim not to have done it. He denies the incident in the face of all of the evidence, either because he wishes he had not done it – and at that age children find it hard to distinguish between reality and fantasy – or because he genuinely cannot remember doing it, or even because he knows he is in trouble and he copies a strategy he has seen others use to get out of the same situation. But to call that 'lying' would be a misnomer. Of course, that does not mean the child's parents should give him a pat on the head for his behaviour. Early incidents like that can be used to explain to the child why it is wrong to say something that is not true, even though he may not fully understand what the fuss is all about. By the age of three or four, however, most children are capable of lying.

A research project examined the effectiveness of different parental reactions to lying. In the study, one set of parents regarded lying simply as something that should be discouraged by prompt punishment, whereas a second set of parents took the view that a child should be taught the distinction between truth and falsehood. This second set of parents used specific incidences of lying to explain moral principles to their young child. Results from the project confirmed that the teaching method is more effective in reducing lying than is the punishment method.

Most parents are unwilling to think that their child might be lying. Often underlying that reluctance is the worry that the child who tells lies in the pre-school years will be a conman as an adult. Yet, there is no evidence to suggest occasionally telling lies as a pre-school child means a future life of deception. Psychological research confirms every child is capable of telling lies, depending on the circumstances.

One investigation into lying used a large room that had a rabbit in a hutch in one corner and a pile of toys, comics and sweets in the opposite corner. Each child individually was taken into the room and was asked to watch the rabbit while the experimenter left for a few moments. After several minutes, the inevitable happened – the lure of the toys and sweets became too much. The child abandoned his assigned task of looking after the rabbit, and instead wandered over to the 'goodies'. As soon as he did that, the experimenter (who was observing the child through the one-way mirror) pressed a switch that made the rabbit disappear through a concealed trapdoor. When the child eventually returned to the corner with the hutch in it, he was shocked to see the rabbit had gone. And at that precise moment the experimenter burst into the room demanding to know what had happened to his rabbit. The children's responses varied from total denial to reluctant admission.

The more forceful the experimenter's inquiry, the less likely the child was to admit negligence. That experiment, and others like it, demonstrated that virtually every child will tell a lie if the situation is threatening enough. The message from these findings is to avoid making a child too fearful or else he will make even greater efforts to justify his lies.

Psychologists once believed honesty and intelligence were positively linked. Many research projects in the 1920s and 1930s did indeed show that children of lower intelligence were more likely to tell lies than were children of higher intelligence. But a likely explanation of this finding is that intelligent children are more capable of lying effectively, and hence are less likely to get caught at it.

Dealing with a child who persists in telling lies can be very frustrating. As well as the general strategies for encouraging moral development, discussed earlier in this chapter, there are several principles that apply specifically to lying:

- *act calmly.* The child genuinely may be confusing fantasy with reality. If that is the case – as it probably will be with a toddler – there is no value in over-reacting.
- *remember that a child may lie in order to cover up something he knows he should not have done.* He lies to avoid detection, not because he wants to add to his list of crimes. In these circumstances, it is best to look on lying as the child's form of self-protection rather than as an attempt by him to be malicious.
- *don't ridicule the child who persists with boastful lies.* His psychological need to lie in this way indicates a lack of self-confidence. Find out from him what he thinks his areas of weakness are, and then aim to improve them so he no longer has the need to brag about himself.

Swearing

Watching a child develop language is one of the rewards of parenthood. You witness the child's progression from mere babbling towards more mature sounds, and then actual words. Then that joy turns to shock when you hear your child unexpectedly cursing and swearing. Bear in mind, though, that the blame for most incidents of foul language by children under the age of five can be laid at the door of parents. You can be sure that the child of that age who swears is merely imitating adult behaviour that he has observed some time earlier. The pre-school child who enters an untidy room, puts his hands on his hips, furrows his brow, and admonishes the occupants with the statement 'What a bloody mess this is!' is acting out a straightforward mimicry of adult behaviour he has already witnessed.

Parental reactions to a toddler's swearing will vary from uncontrollable laughter to a severe telling-off. The best way to deal with an incident of swearing at this age is to ignore it – and make sure that people don't swear in front of the child in the future. If you do draw undue attention to swearing, then the manipulative toddler will soon realize that a swear-word is a special word with a special effect – and that it is a good way to get your attention. That awareness will simply encourage the child to repeat the word.

The child of school age is often attracted to swear-words precisely because he knows these are words used by adults. He thinks that by adopting grown-up mannerisms, then he will become more grown-up himself. The guidelines given earlier in this chaper to promote your child's moral awareness also apply to swearing. In particular, explain to the child that his swearing will mean that some parents will not let their children play with him. Never tell a child that swearing is only something adults are allowed to do.

Encouraging moral behaviour

Rather than concentrating solely on ways to stop a child behaving antisocially – a bit like closing the stable door after the horse has bolted – you can adopt a more positive approach by considering ways to encourage your child to behave pro-socially.

- *behave responsibly yourself*. A study compared two groups of children. The first group spent a long time with an adult who was caring, altruistic and who adhered to rules. The second group spent the same amount of time in the presence of an adult who remained aloof, uncaring and unresponsive. The results indicated that children in the first group were far more likely to be altruistic and morally mature than were children in the latter group. Your child can learn pro-social behaviour by modelling himself on your example.
- *give your child tasks that involve responsibility*. One project

looked at the extent to which a child would act responsibly towards a younger child in distress. Researchers found that a child was much more likely to comfort a tearful infant if he had been 'officially' told he was responsible for her. Where a child had not been given that responsibility, he was unlikely to be responsive to her distress. Giving a child small assignments, with a degree of responsibility attached, will encourage pro-social behaviour.

- *ask your child to teach moral behaviour to a younger child.* It appears that a child's moral behaviour will be enhanced by teaching what he already knows to another child; for instance, where a child has shown a younger child how to share toys and sweets, both children appear to be better at sharing.

Chapter 17

Socialization

Getting on with others is so important. A sociable child has so many advantages compared to a child who does not mix well. The ability to relate to other people gives a child self-confidence, it allows her to have varied social experiences, and it results in a more stimulating way of life. There are, of course, children who deliberately choose to lead a solitary life, and they appear to be very contented, but in most instances an isolated child is an unhappy child. And societies function more effectively when people are able to co-operate with each other, when they can share things with each other, and when they are able to take another person's point of view.

Children seem to have an inborn ability to relate to others. Indeed, a baby could not possibly survive without the capacity to accept love and care from someone else. The very early emotional attachments between parent and baby form the basis for the child's future social relationships. (This is discussed in more detail in Chapter 4.) Children who have not formed a secure emotional bond with at least one adult within the first few years of life often find social relationships difficult in later life.

What makes a child popular

Numerous studies have shown that popular children, compared with unpopular children, tend to be:

- *academically capable:* they do well in school, and gain high marks in exams
- *physically attractive:* unfair as it may seem, the more a child's appearance conforms to the prevailing concept of 'good-looking', then the more popular she is likely to be
- *mature:* children who are physically and emotionally mature tend to be more popular than less mature children
- *youngest children:* first-born children are frequently less popular than youngest children in a family
- *athletic:* a child with good sporting ability is more likely to be popular than a physically inept child.

Now there is little you can do about these qualities. Your child either does or does not fall into such categories. However, popularity also depends on a child's command of social skills. Despite an inherent tendency towards social involvement, children still need to learn how to behave in ways that will make them popular. Having these 'social' skills is no guarantee of instant popularity, but they go a long way towards it. The main ones are:

- *communication:* anti-social behaviour often stems from a child's inability to communicate her emotions and desires through spoken language. The child who has learned to express her feelings by making the statement 'I want to play with that toy once you have finished with it' will be more socially acceptable than the child who simply goes up and grabs the toy out of her friend's hands without any explanation. You can enhance your child's communication skills by encouraging her to voice her feelings instead of acting them out impulsively. When suitable opportunities arise, ask your child questions about how she is feeling, and what she is thinking. That gets her into the habit of using words, rather than actions, to communicate.
- *social confidence:* the first few moments in any social encounter between children are often the most difficult, and the child who is confident enough to cope with these opening moments is likely to get on better with others. Teach your

Understanding Children

child some 'opening strategies' for use when she first meets new children, for instance, that she should ask the other child to play a game, or she should ask the other child about his favourite television programme. Let your child practise these techniques in role-play situations with you at home. (This is discussed in more detail in Chapter 10.)

- *pacifying gestures:* some gestures that children make can be described as aggressive (shouting, scowling, clenching fists, swearing) while other gestures can be described as pacifying (smiling, showing approval, offering a toy, holding out a hand). Research confirms that children who mix well are usually those children who use more pacifying gestures than aggressive gestures. Encourage your child to adopt these habits.
- *sharing:* at some point during play, a child will be asked by her friend to share her toys, and a child unwilling to do this will find play situations stressful. Only children often find sharing especially difficult because they are so used to having everything for themselves. Teach your child how to share, using two methods. First, explain to her why she should share. Use reasons that are meaningful to her, for instance, that sharing gives everyone a turn, that other children will like her if she shares her toys, and so on. Second, teach sharing by example. When you see your child arguing with her friend over who is allowed to play with a particular toy, you may be tempted to remove the object altogether as a punishment. But this will only teach the child to fight quietly without attracting your attention. Far better to show the child that one of them can play with the toy for a few minutes, then the other can. Once a child is able to share, she will be more relaxed in a play situation because she does not have to worry all the time about hanging on doggedly to her possessions.
- *turn-taking:* children cannot possibly play games successfully without being able to take turns. But a young child is only concerned with herself, and the ability to wait while others receive attention first does not come naturally. This has to be learned. There are many opportunities at home for teaching

this social skill to your child. Waiting her turn to tell her father some piece of news, or waiting till her brother gets a cup of juice before she does, allows your child to experience turn-taking as a normal part of social interactions.
- *following rules:* a child cannot join in games with her friends unless she is able to follow the rules. As with all social skills, this can be taught at home. Play games that involve rules with your child. Explain to your child why games have rules and why they should be followed. If she learns this through playing with you, then the chances are she will be able to apply this to playing games with her friends.
- *positive reinforcement:* close investigation of children playing has revealed that a child who gives positive reinforcement to other children will have a higher level of social acceptance. So encourage your child to show approval of her friends, and to praise them when they do things that she likes. These simple strategies will enhance her ability to mix appropriately with others.
- *cleanliness:* a grubby child will have social difficulties. Life is unfair, and although it is not a child's fault if she has dirty clothes or is unwashed – those are the parents' responsibility – the child with a poor level of hygiene has an uphill struggle when it comes to mixing with others. A child needs to be shown basic standards of health care, such as caring for her clothes, brushing her hair, washing her hands after going to the toilet, brushing her teeth in the morning and at night, and so on. Most children will take the easy way out in matters of hygiene if left to their own devices, and so you have to encourage your child to take an interest in her appearance. Looking presentable goes a long way towards being socially acceptable.

Eating habits and popularity

There are few aspects of behaviour more likely to discourage friendships than sloppy eating habits. A school-age child who has disgusting table manners will find herself surrounded by empty seats during mealtimes, and the stigma may well carry

Understanding Children

into play. There is, however, no point in trying to teach your child how to behave at mealtimes before she is old enough to understand what is going on.

A young baby has no table manners. She is not bothered at all about the mess she makes, or whether her eating habits cause discomfort to anyone else. All she cares about is that she can consume her milk as quickly as possible. Later on, when she is slightly older and more able to use her hands and arms, a baby regards food as having play value. The inquisitive toddler wants to see if her breakfast cereal sticks to the walls, if it trickles through her fingers, if it makes a mark on her clothes, or even if throwing it will bring attention from her mother and father.

The twelve-month-old child still regards mealtimes as periods for explorations, but you can begin to encourage a child of that age to develop some control over her hand movements. Gaining control over cutlery – a skill you may take for granted – takes time to acquire. As an approximate guide, a baby of just under a year will probably use her fingers to feed herself, and will make an effort to help hold her cup while drinking from it. By around eighteen months, a child may be able to manage a cup on her own, using both hands. And the typical toddler of twenty-four months can use a spoon and a fork for eating, although she is likely to create a bit of a mess in the process. The average three-year-old child is able to use a spoon and fork more capably, while at four or five the child will be able to use a knife and fork at mealtimes. At each stage of development, your child needs encouragement to gain better control over her eating habits, and she may prefer to remain at her current level rather than face the prospect of learning a new feeding skill. With lots of practice and help from parents, most children gain reasonable hand control for mealtimes. In doing so, the child enhances her ability to socialize.

A child learns how to behave by copying the other members of her family. If your table manners are satisfactory, then it is likely that your child will imitate this style of behaviour at the table. On the other hand, if you belch your way through lunch, you should not be surprised when your child behaves in a similar way. Children imitate the negative aspects of their parents' behaviour as well as the positive aspects. Set a good example yourself.

Parent behaviour and popularity

Irrespective of all of these personal habits, psychologists have demonstrated that a child's popularity is also affected by the way she is brought up at home. Studies confirm that parents of popular children, when compared with parents of unpopular children:

- discourage anti-social and aggressive behaviour at home
- discipline their children through praise and reward for good behaviour rather than punishment or deprivation of privileges for bad behaviour
- have warm relationships between members of the family and express affection quite openly
- give reasons to their child when encouraging her to behave appropriately
- have strong feelings of self-confidence about their own roles as parents
- encourage their child to achieve a reasonable degree of independence within the home and outside
- have greater agreement with each other about the way the children should be managed

Friendships

Children form friendships for many different reasons. At times it is difficult for parents to discern why two children enjoy each other's company so much. Friendships provide psychological benefits, such as giving a child self-confidence, giving her someone to share her secrets with, teaching her about the significance of loyalty, and offering her the experience of sharing with another child. Friendships can also serve practical purposes, such as allowing a child to have access to her friend's toys. Many friendships in the pre-school years are motivated more by this type of pragmatic self-interest than by strong feelings of personal attraction. What you as an adult look for in a friendship may well differ from what your child looks for in her friends.

Research studies have shown certain patterns in children's friendships:

- school-age children tend to select friends of the same sex, though not always.
- children tend to pick friends who are at the same level of emotional and social maturity and who have similar personality characteristics as themselves.
- children do not necessarily choose friends who are as intelligent as themselves.
- only children are more capable of sustaining friendships for a longer period than are children from large families.
- girls appear to be more sociable than boys; they find it easier to make friends in new social situations.
- capable and energetic children rarely select lethargic and unresponsive children to be their friends.
- among ten-year-olds, the most common reason given for having a particular child as a friend is the fact that they live close to each other or that they see each other every day. The next most common reason is that the friend likes the same types of activity and has the same interests.
- friendships among pre-school children fluctuate from week to week because at that age a child is very self-centred. It is not until the child is nine or ten that she begins to form long-lasting stable friendships.
- inability to form friendships may be an indication of an emotional disturbance, though this is uncommon.

Problems arise when parents disapprove of their child's friend because she behaves in ways that are not acceptable by their standards. This requires delicate and tactful handling. Never forbid your child to play with another child in her class, or in the neighbourhood, since this will only have the opposite effect to that actually desired – forbidden fruit is always more exciting. Honesty with your child is the best approach in this situation. Tell your child why it is that she should not play with her friend (for instance, because she uses bad language, or because she gets into trouble for being naughty). Don't keep repeating everything you think is wrong with her friend, or your child will consider you are being totally unfair in your judgement. Give a balanced view. If you find that your child persists in playing with that friend despite your admonitions (and this will probably happen when both children are in the same school) emphasize to your child that although she and her friend play together that does not mean she has to behave in the same way as her friend.

A more positive approach when trying to discourage one friendship is actively to encourage another. Focus your child's time and attention on to an alternative friendship. The younger the child is, then the easier this is to do. Invite other children whom you do regard as suitable company for your child to the house to play. In the end, your child is still going to make up her own mind about whom she wants to play with, but your persistent attempts to nurture particular friendships may pay off eventually.

Fighting

Your management of your child's aggression at home affects her ability to interact with other children without fighting with them. (This is discussed in more detail in Chapter 6.) Yet minor fights between children are a normal part of everyday life. Fights start because a child:

- feels her authority is threatened by another child and so she fights her to show she is in charge
- has become extremely confident and wants to show she is more capable than anyone else
- is very competitive and wants to win at all costs
- is encouraged by her parents to stand up for herself when compromised by other children

Understanding Children

- is in a bad mood and releases her anger by picking on an innocent bystander
- has her toys or possessions taken away by another child without any explanation

The reality of childhood arguments is that the strongest fighter most often gets her own way, and you will have a hard time convincing your child she should not fight when she sees other children use that technique effectively. Assuming you do not approve of aggressive antisocial behaviour, you have to teach your child other ways of coping with conflict, ways that don't involve physical or verbal assault on other children. Suggestions for this include:

- *compromise:* fights often develop when two children desire an object at the same time. One way round this is for the children to reach a compromise so that both have access to what they want. For instance, when children disagree over what game to play, suggest to them that they play one game first, then the other. Emphasize that this type of compromise is not the same as giving in because in the end both children will get what they want. Tell them this is a more sensible way of settling disputes. The best timing for compromises is before the disagreement has escalated into a full-scale conflict.
- *discussions:* encourage your child to talk about her conflicts, to explain why she feels angry about something. The more she does this then the less likely she is to act impulsively in anger. The child who is able to talk her way out of trouble will find life much less traumatic.
- *distractions:* conflict can be avoided by distracting the aggressor. Many adults use this technique successfully and there is no reason why a child should not do the same. Distraction involves attracting the hostile child's attention to some other matter, such as telling her that an adult is about to walk into the room. This is an effective way of breaking tension.

Some parents may feel these strategies simply encourage their child to be weak, to be afraid of aggressive children. Instead they would prefer their child to be able to face up to conflict. Other parents may feel that all conflicts should be resolved as amicably as possible. It is a matter of personal choice.

Bullying

Bullying is one of the worst forms of antisocial behaviour. It involves exploiting someone else's personal weakness by frightening them into acquiescence. There are children who are raised in an environment where rough-and-tumble play is accepted as normal, and when these children play with others at school they may be a lot more physical in their play than their friends. But that is not bullying, because the behaviour of such children lacks a malicious and sinister dimension. Bullying is a deliberate act of coercion.

There can be different explanations for a bully's behaviour. The most likely one is that she has seen her parents behave this way, either towards herself or towards each other, and the child is modelling her own behaviour on that. Bullying parents are likely to have bullying children. A less common explanation for bullying is that the bully feels she is inferior; to compensate for this feeling of inadequacy, she tries to prove she is capable by exerting her authority over other children. This may explain why some physically small children are bullies.

Sometimes a child bullies because she cannot relate to children in any other way. Bullying allows her to have some contact with others – even though that contact has a negative quality. And there are children who bully as a result of their unhappiness, stemming either from a troubled home life or from a troubled school life.

If your child regularly comes home complaining she is being bullied by one particular child, spend some time considering whether your child's own behaviour is contributing to the amount of bullying she is experiencing. This is not a matter of blaming the victim – some children unconsciously invite others to abuse them. In order to determine whether this applies to your child, ask yourself the following questions:

Understanding Children

- *does she get bullied by more than one child?* While there is likely to be one bully among the children she mixes with, there are not likely to be several.
- *has she shown attention-seeking behaviour in other ways?* If your child is regularly attention-seeking, then bullying may be another means of achieving this purpose.
- *do you find you are constantly reprimanding her at home?* Your child may be unconsciously encouraging others to bully her as a form of punishment for the guilt she feels.

Most children are reluctant to admit they are being bullied and so you should take your child's complaints seriously. It has probably taken a great deal of courage for your child to have raised this issue with you. Your first reaction might be to approach the bully's parents in order to ask them to exercise more control over their child. Your own child will probably discourage you from doing this for fear of retaliation. A more effective technique is to teach your child how to cope on her own with bullying. Consider the following suggestions:

- *tell your child to avoid the bully whenever possible:* when approached by the bully, your child should walk away without saying anything – preferably to somewhere safe. That is not an act of cowardice.
- *persuade your child to show no reaction whatsoever to the bully's behaviour:* the less upset your child appears to be then the less likely is the bully to repeat her actions. Your child will not find this easy but you could practise through role-play situations at home.
- *boost your child's self-confidence:* emphasize her strong points and explain that the bully is picking on her because she is jealous of her. By all means teach her self-defence skills in the hope of making her feel confident when facing a bully, but bear in mind that she is unlikely to become proficient in a short time and might mistakenly assume she can beat the bully – a situation that could backfire on her.

Chapter 18

Discipline

Discipline is an essential part of parenthood. Caring and sensitive discipline helps a child because:

- it provides a structure and consistency in a child's life
- it sets out clear standards of behaviour for a child to follow
- it encourages him to consider other people's feelings
- it makes a child feel safe and secure.

There are many different ways of administering discipline in the family. For example, the Victorians believed discipline should be very strict and that children should do absolutely everything that they were told. The typical Victorian father would not tolerate any challenge to his authority and his children's independence was discouraged. Other parents believe discipline should be administered under the principle 'spare the rod and spoil the child' – in other words, discipline means physical punishment every time the child breaks a rule. And then there are some parents who believe the only way for a child to learn how to behave is through self-discipline. Instead of forcing their child to conform to rules, these parents encourage their child to learn acceptable standards of behaviour by himself, from his own experiences. Each type of discipline has its own distinct effect on the child's development.

When discipline should begin

The process of understanding rules begins very early on in a child's life. When a baby is born, there are certain actions that he does automatically, by reflex, such as crying when he is hungry and grasping when something is placed in the palm of his hand. These acts of behaviour occur instinctively without the child's having to think about them. Yet most things that children do have to be learned. And that includes discipline. But psychologists disagree over when discipline should start.

Some think a baby is so small that he cannot be expected to follow rules because he does not understand what is going on around him. These professionals believe parents should respond to their baby whenever he cries. Others think that discipline should start at birth, and that the undisciplined baby will turn into an undisciplined child. These professionals firmly believe that a rigorous feeding, sleeping and changing routine should be followed at all times.

There is no 'right' answer to this, although there is no point in disciplining a child who is too young to understand what it is you are trying to achieve. Certainly a young baby can learn that crying is a good way of getting his parents' attention, and many parents find themselves totally exhausted when they fall into the pattern of responding to their baby every time he cries. Yet failure to respond can also be detrimental to the baby's development. Consistent refusal to react positively to a crying baby teaches him that he is not very important. It communicates the message that although he is unhappy his parents are not going to do anything to relieve his distress. Repeated experiences like that will reduce his feelings of security and he may cry more frequently as a result.

Even so, a child needs consistency in his life. So you have to strike a balance between rushing to your baby every time he whimpers and ignoring him when he cries between meals. By around nine months, a child understands what you mean when you say 'no' to him. At that point, the process of establishing discipline begins.

Administering discipline

You have to decide for yourself what style of discipline you feel most comfortable with in your family. Every family is unique, but there are certain 'dos' and 'don'ts' applicable to everyone:

DO

- *remember that discipline helps your child's development;* it has many positive aspects and is not just a system of rules for controlling him. Don't lose sight of this – it will reassure you of the purpose behind your actions.
- *present rules to your child in a caring and sensitive way;* he is much more likely to listen to what you have to say if he thinks you are establishing discipline because you love him than if he thinks you have rules because you cannot be bothered with him.
- *explain to your child why rules matter;* use terms that he can understand, for instance, that taking his friend's toy away without asking would upset him. A child is more likely to follow rules when he can see sense underlying them.
- *use discipline to teach your child to behave appropriately when he is outside the family home;* if he thinks that there is one set of rules for home and another for elsewhere, he will adjust his behaviour accordingly. When he comes home from a friend's house, ask him how he behaved. Praise him when he shows self-discipline in the company of others, and show your disapproval when he misbehaves.
- *emphasize that he will benefit from rules just as much as anyone else;* remind him that rules are reciprocal. For instance, the rule that children do not throw stones at each other means he will not be hit by a stone thrown by another child.
- *keep your family rules consistent;* inconsistency confuses a child. Everybody needs some structure and predictability in life, and so discipline has to be established consistently. Although there are times when your household rules should be flexible, in most cases if parental limits have been set the child should be expected to follow them.

Understanding Children

- *be prepared to take action if your child regularly breaks the rules;* if you have made it clear to your child that he will be punished in a specific way for breaking a specific rule, then stick to what you have said. Empty threats simply teach a child that his mother and father do not mean what they say.
- *make punishments realistic and meaningful to your child;* the most effective form of punishment is one that the child regards negatively, not necessarily the one you regard negatively. Telling your child that he has to go to bed ten minutes early because he threw his dinner on the floor will be more effective than saying he will never be given dinner again – indeed, at that moment, he would probably be delighted never to sit through the evening meal again.
- *time punishments properly;* using rewards and punishments to reinforce your discipline is most effective if they are given immediately after the behaviour has occurred. The longer the time between your child's actions and your own response, then the less effective is your discipline.
- *use rewards to encourage your child to abide by your standards;* praise your child when he is behaving well. There is no harm in giving the older child a special treat as a reward for having a particularly good day. That will encourage him to follow rules in the future.
- *avoid nagging at your child;* easier said than done, but you are likely to feel miserable at the end of a day during which you have nagged your child constantly to behave. Nagging simply teaches a child to ignore what you say, because he knows you are going to go on and on and on.
- *set a good example of behaviour yourself;* you cannot realistically expect your child to behave differently from the way you do, and therefore be sure that you can justify your actions to the child if he should ever ask about them.
- *accept that your child will challenge your authority from time to time;* that struggle for independence is a normal – though extremely infuriating – part of your child's development. The child will probably make his first serious challenge to your standards of discipline when he reaches the age of two or three. By that stage, he begins to realize that he can do

Discipline

things on his own – he does not need to rely on you so much and, by definition, he does not need your authority. That is when tantrums emerge. Eventually, however, this phase passes and your child will settle down to acquire a more reasonable attitude to discipline.
- *be prepared to say you are sorry;* there will be times when you discipline your child and then you find out you are wrong. That happens to every parent, and when it does the parent has nothing to fear in saying sorry. Admitting your own fallibility in front of your child is not a sign of weakness. On the contrary, it will encourage him by example to be honest in recognizing his own mistakes.

DON'T

- *try to bully your child into good behaviour;* of course you are bigger than he is and you can momentarily intimidate him into doing what you want. But the effect will be only temporary, and his unresponsiveness to discipline will emerge as soon as he is out of your sight. In addition, bullying him only sets a bad example; it leads to confrontation and it will encourage him to be aggressive.
- *suggest to your child that he should follow a rule simply because a grown-up tells him to;* he has to learn to differentiate between right and wrong, and the instruction to do whatever he is told by an adult does not encourage him to be discriminating. As well as that, your child should be treated with respect, not coerced into behaviour without explanation.
- *threaten your child with overly severe punishments that you would not be prepared to carry out anyway;* in moments of temper you may be tempted to tell your child that he will never be allowed to play outside again, but you will never follow that threat through. And that will teach him that your discipline can be rejected without punishment. It will be far more meaningful, for example, to deprive your child of ten minutes of television viewing.
- *repeatedly smack your child for continual misbehaviour;* that will only make him more disruptive, more aggressive, and less

amenable to your discipline. Find a more suitable punishment, such as putting him to bed early, or withdrawing his sweets, and so on.
- *be afraid to reach a compromise with your child;* sometimes your child will want to break a family rule because that is the only way he can develop his independence, and you should be prepared to compromise with him. No rule should be so inflexible that it cannot ever bend. If you are prepared to reach a compromise over specific matters, then that reminds your child that he, too, will have to compromise sometimes.
- *get into conflicts with your child that you cannot win;* there are some areas of behaviour that you cannot control unless your child co-operates fully with you, for instance, feeding, sleeping or using the toilet. No parent can force a child to eat food that is in front of him, to go to sleep when he is told, or to empty his bladder and bowels on demand. So do not use these aspects of behaviour as testing grounds for your discipline.

Spoiling a child

Lack of discipline can result in a spoiled child, who is over-indulged, strong-willed and who expects to get his own way every time no matter what anyone else wants. A spoiled child exercises control over his parents (not the other way round as is usually the case in parent–child relationships) and is uncooperative when things don't go his way. This type of child is rarely happy because he always wants more than he already has. And he will not be popular because he will be unable to take turns in games, or let others choose what activities to play at, or share his toys.

No parent deliberately sets out to encourage a child to have all these undesirable qualities. Instead, spoiling seems to be one of these processes that creep up on parents without their noticing until someone points it out. By then, however, the pattern of spoiling is well established and the child will strongly resist any parental desire for change. That means

Discipline

that a spoiled young child will develop into a spoiled older child. Even though you may not want to spoil your child, you might find these wishes being undermined by the child's grandparents. Many people regard presents as being synonymous with love, and so grandparents often reason that the more presents they give, then the more they must love the child. Do not be afraid to put your foot down if you want to discourage this.

Avoiding spoiling

Spoiling is not just simply what material goods a child has, nor is it simply a matter of what he is allowed to do. The way a child is managed by his parents is what matters. Strategies to avoid spoiling include:

- *make sure there are some occasions when your child does not get what he wants:* even if your child has an abundance of toys, clothes and presents, ensure there are times when he is denied something that he asks for. That teaches him how to cope with situations that do not go the way he wants. The relative balance between when a child gets what he wants and when he does not get what he wants is more important than the absolute amount of things that he gets.
- *encourage your child to justify why he wants something;* it is very easy to accede to your child's requests simply because it means you will have a quiet life – but the act of acquisition, however, quickly becomes intrinsically more important to the child than the actual enjoyment of having the object. Getting a child to explain why he wants something encourages him to think about what is going on.
- *be prepared to compromise between what you want and what your child wants;* if your son is agitated because he can't get the large boat he has seen in the toy shop, explain to him that he will have to wait until his birthday to get it, or that he can have a smaller boat. Always tell your child why you are not letting him have what he wants.
- *explain to your child about understanding other people's point of*

Understanding Children

view; young children, spoiled or not, only see the world from their own perspective, and they need to be encouraged to think about others' feelings. For instance, when he has punched another child because he came last in the game, talk to him about what the other child must feel. Of course, when you do this your child is probably disinterested in what you say, but if you do take this approach regularly, your message should get through eventually.

- *let your child make minor decisions about his life*; a child who is given some control over his day-to-day routine does not feel the need to exercise authority over his parents.

Chapter 19

Children with Special Needs

All children have a range of psychological needs; the need to be loved, the need to be physically cared for, the need to feel secure, the need to have self-confidence, the need to have structure and consistency in life and the need to mix with other children. A child whose psychological needs are not met will experience emotional difficulties. For instance, a child who is not loved will have difficulty forming stable relationships in adulthood. A child who is denied the opportunity to mix with other children will experience later difficulty in establishing social relationships. And a child brought up in an environment of instability at home will be unable to cope with the demands of school. It is your job as a parent to ensure that your child's psychological needs are satisfied.

But there are some children who have special needs in addition to those described above, needs that arise because the child has atypical development. Until this decade, psychologists and child-care professionals described these children as 'handicapped' or 'subnormal'. So a child who was paralysed from the waist down, or who had weak muscles, or who required crutches to move around, was described as 'physically handicapped'; a child who was completely blind, or who had limited vision in both eyes, or who had cataracts, was described as 'visually handicapped'; and a child who could not keep up with her school work, or who had Down's Syndrome, or who failed to learn to speak, or who never developed enough to be able to sit up unsupported, was described as 'mentally handicapped' or 'mentally subnormal'. These labels were used to identify and categorize children with developmental problems.

This form of labelling is no longer used. Now, children with developmental problems are described as having 'special needs'. This change in terminology, though, is not simply a substitution of one label for another. It occurred for the following reasons:

- the terms 'handicapped' or 'subnormal' do not reveal anything about the child's strengths, only her weaknesses. They indicate that she has something wrong with her, but not the practical effect of the difficulty. A child may be unable to walk, and yet might be confident and determined, able to use elbow crutches to move around the room. Labelling this child 'physically handicapped' focuses on her physical difficulty only, and tells nothing of how she is coping with that difficulty.
- the terms 'handicapped' or 'subnormal' are too general, and fail to recognize essential differences between children. They suggest that all 'handicapped' or 'subnormal' children are the same, and need the same sort of help. Yet that is not the case. One child might find school work so difficult that she cannot learn in normal-sized classes and requires individual teaching. Another child might be unable to feed and toilet herself, and be unable to speak except with monosyllabic grunts. Labelling both these children as 'mentally handicapped' or 'mentally subnormal' fails to differentiate the individual level of development that each child has.
- the terms 'handicapped' or 'subnormal' suggest the difficulties are all-or-none, that a child is either handicapped or she is not handicapped. There is no such clear-cut division. Child development occurs on a continuum from normality to abnormality, and virtually all children lie at a point between these two extremes. Children with special features therefore share many common features with all children. Labelling a child as 'handicapped' or 'subnormal' suggests she is radically different from other children, when in fact

Children with Special Needs

she is simply at a different point in the same developmental continuum.
- the terms 'handicapped' or 'subnormal' do not indicate what sort of measures would help the child overcome, or at least cope with, her developmental difficulty. They only state that she has a problem. Two children may be 'visually handicapped', but one might have no vision at all and needs to learn braille, whereas another child might have limited vision and needs to read using magnifiers. Labelling both these children as 'visually handicapped' fails to say what specific help these children need.
- the terms 'handicapped' or 'subnormal' encourage people to focus on the child's condition, rather than on the child herself as an individual. They suggest there is homogeneity among children with special needs. That is far from the truth. For instance, many people assume that all children with Down's Syndrome are the same because they have very similar facial features and ostensibly similar levels of development. Yet if you have the opportunity to get to know a child with this genetic condition, you will soon realize that the child is a unique individual with her own personality, her own ideas, her own sense of humour and her own level of abilities. She is a child, not a combination of genes. Labelling the child 'Down's Syndrome' is an accurate description of her genetic condition, but it encourages people to view her in stereotyped ways.

Shifting the emphasis away from 'handicap' (considering the child's weaknesses only) to 'special needs' (considering ways in which the child can be supported so that her development is least impaired by her difficulty) allows each child to be treated as an individual. It is also more likely to lead to the child receiving the necessary help.

Raising a child with special needs

The following guidelines may be helpful for parents of a child with special needs:

- *find out as much as you can about your child's difficulty and the possible impact it might have on her development;* realizing your child has special needs is upsetting and you will take time to adjust. But the feelings of worry many parents have stem from lack of knowledge of the child's likely future development. Ask the professionals who you are involved with, whether a psychologist, paediatrician, geneticist, physiotherapist or speech therapist. Request specific information from those working with your child. Many parents with a special-needs child complain that they never get a 'straight answer' from professionals or that they never have enough time with them to ask questions. Be prepared to persist with your enquiries.
- *if you don't have confidence in those professionals who are supervising your child's development, ask to be referred to someone else;* you will have close involvement with a child psychologist and probably with a paediatrician. If you feel uncomfortable with any of these professionals, or you feel unable to trust their judgement, or if you lack confidence in them, ask to be referred to someone else. You are entitled to do that, and no professional would feel satisfied working with a client who felt ill at ease with him.
- *contact other parents who have a child with difficulties similar to those of your child;* you will benefit from sharing your worries with someone else, and you will be able to pool your experiences. This can usually be done through organizations specifically formed to help parents. Many parents find this form of optional contact useful in clarifying their understanding of their child's development.
- *remember that your child with special needs has the same psychological needs as other children;* she needs just as much love, security, care, acceptance and comfort. She also needs structure in her life. You may be tempted to 'spoil' her because of the difficulties she is experiencing, but long-term over-indulgence will not be in her best interests. (This is discussed in more detail in Chapter 18.)
- *bring up your special-needs child in a way that maximizes her potential, as you would with any other child in the family;* all

parents want their child to achieve to the fullest of her ability, whether the achievements are at school, with friends, on the sports field, in music, or in art – and the same should apply to a child with special needs. No matter the extent of her limitations, the child needs to be given opportunities that will encourage her full development.
- *try to adjust to uncertainty;* although very general predictions can be made about a child's future on the basis of very early development, specific predictions are virtually impossible to make. This means that many of the questions you want to ask about your special-needs child – such as if she will ever be able to talk, if she will ever walk by herself, or if she will require special education – cannot be answered with any certainty until the child is older.
- *don't assume that because your child has special needs that somehow she has a natural affinity to interact with other children who have special needs;* this common assumption has absolutely no evidence to support it. Your special-needs child should be given as much opportunity as possible to mix with other children of normal development, in local playgroups or nurseries. Resist the temptation to provide her with only protected play experiences. There is a place in the child's life for interacting with all types of children.
- *remember that there is a difference between a disability and an impairment;* a disability only becomes an impairment when it seriously interferes with the child's development. A physically disabled child can lead an active and stimulating life, minimizing the effect of her disability. However, parents of a physically disabled child may be so protective that the child's self-confidence is reduced to the point where she shows little motivation to do anything for herself. When that happens, the disability has a negative impact on all aspects of the child's development, thereby becoming an impairment. Your behaviour towards your child is a determining factor in the effect of her developmental problem.

Schooling for a child with special needs

Until recently, children with special needs have been educated in segregated special schools. These schools – often situated in isolation away from ordinary schools – offer smaller classes, more experienced and specially trained teachers, auxiliary staff to provide the child with additional help in non-educational tasks, and possibly specialist physiotherapy and speech therapy. Those additional facilities allow the child to receive a specialized curriculum tailored to her individual educational needs. Extra teacher attention means the child can be given more help than she could in an ordinary primary school class.

Yet decades of segregated special schooling have produced remarkably little experimental evidence to suggest children with special needs progress any better in these schools than they do in ordinary schools. Indeed, one of the drawbacks of segregated special schools is that they reduce the child's involvement with normal children – and this can impair the child's social development.

The combination of these factors has reversed the trend of special schooling. Now, many child psychologists seek to integrate a child with special needs into her local school before considering the possibility of a segregated special school. Of course, there are some children whose development is so severely impaired, to the point where they require constant care, that their needs could never be met in an ordinary school. However, there is an increasing awareness that many children with special needs can cope in their local school as long as they are given the necessary support. There is no reason why a child with learning difficulties should have to attend a special school in order to receive individual teacher attention. A remedial teacher could visit the local school regularly, providing additional support when required. In most cases a child's special needs can be met in the ordinary school if adequate resources are provided. Likewise, there is no reason why a pupil in a wheelchair, for instance, should not attend her local school. If the school is flat, having been built on the level, then it will be ideal. If the school has some steps, then a ramp can be fitted by the local authority for very little cost. Should the child need physiotherapy, this can be given at her home after school hours. This reduces the justification for segregating special-needs pupils from others.

Local education authorities are more ready to accept this principle of integration, and are increasingly willing to support special-needs pupils in local schools. For example, in the past Down's Syndrome children were automatically placed in special schools but there are now many instances of Down's Syndrome children being educated in their local schools. And they are making progress. Some local authorities are even starting the process of integration at the nursery stage, which makes integration at the primary stage easier.

As a parent, you may feel your child with special needs would be better off at a segregated special school, with its guaranteed extra resources and its protective environment. You may reject the idea of integration on the basis that the child will not receive the help she needs, and that she will be abused by the other children in the school. That is your decision. At least parents are now being offered a choice. Make your choice of schooling only after detailed consideration of which school can best meet your child's educational, social and psychological needs.

A special-needs child in the family

By necessity, a child with special needs becomes the focus of her family. This is perfectly understandable. Practical circumstances dictate this and the parents have little choice in the matter. Of course, parents of a special-needs child are under tremendous pressure, but they usually receive help. There will be psychologists and paediatricians, social workers and welfare officers, health visitors and physiotherapists, all willing to support the stressed mother and father. The danger, however, is that the other children in the family may get left out. All children need parental attention.

Psychological research confirms that when a child in the

family has special needs, the other children (compared with those in families where there is not a special-needs child):

- have a higher level of antisocial behaviour
- are more likely to have a mild emotional difficulty
- may be anxious that they themselves will develop the same condition as the child with special needs
- are expected by their parents to take on more domestic responsibilities
- assume they will have full responsibility for the special-needs child when their parents die
- often feel neglected
- frequently complain that their parents expect them to do exceptionally well at school
- experience parental pressure to be 'normal'.

The way a child reacts to a brother or sister with special needs depends on several factors. First, there is the child's age. A child several years older than the special-needs child will have been aware of the difficulties right from the beginning, and will have been involved from the time the child was brought home from the maternity hospital. Yet a child younger than the special-needs child is unlikely to show any real understanding until she reaches school age. By missing out on the early adjustment the family had to make, the child's awareness takes longer to develop. Second, there is the sex of the child. It appears that girls are more likely to be adversely affected by the presence of a child with special needs in the family than are boys. An explanation of this finding is that girls are usually given more family responsibilities than boys and therefore are more likely to feel the special-needs child's presence as a burden. Third, there is the severity of the difficulties: the greater the special-needs child's impairment, then the greater the impact on other children in the family.

If you have a child with special needs in your family, when dealing with your other children:

- *encourage them to communicate with each other about the child's*

abnormalities; research suggests this type of communication among children in a family does not often happen spontaneously. Let them talk about the effect the child with special needs has on them personally.
- *give them information about the nature of the child's difficulty;* anxiety frequently stems from misunderstanding or lack of knowledge of the condition affecting their brother or sister.
- *pitch any discussion of special needs at a level the children can understand;* use terms that are meaningful. Although a child may not grasp the meaning of 'brain damage', she will understand 'unable to learn to read'. Likewise, a child will grasp the idea of 'unable to run' more easily than she will grasp the idea of 'spinal deformity'. Even limited explanations are better than none at all.
- *let them express their feelings openly and honestly;* it is not a crime to admit fear at having a brother who is blind, or embarrassment at having a slow-learning sister. Ignoring these worries will not make them go away. A more effective strategy is to let the children come to terms with these feelings, through candid discussion within a caring family environment.
- *involve them in the care of the special-needs child;* research has found that when the children are allowed to become involved in the day-to-day management of the child with special needs – without being given overwhelming responsibility – their self-esteem improves, as does their pride in their brother's or sister's achievements.

Every child is special

All the children in your family have their own lives to lead, not just the child with special needs. Do not cover up the child's special needs, but do not make them a permanent and all-encompassing focus for the whole family. A balanced perspective lets every child benefit from individual parental love and attention.

Developmental Checklists

Every child develops at her own rate. What one child can do at a specific age, another child the same age may not be able to do. For instance, the 'average' age that an infant is able to sit upright by herself without support is between six and nine months. Some are able to do this at six months while others cannot until nine months. Similarly, the average age at which a child begins to put two words together to form a phrase is around eighteen months, but many toddlers do not reach this stage until twenty-four months, or even older. In most cases, these individual differences are normal and are no cause for concern.

Checklist-type scales of development – such as those outlined in this chapter – are helpful for parents as well as psychologists precisely because they give some guidelines as to the approximate rate of development. Bear in mind though:

- there is no such being as the 'average child', who reaches every stage just at the time expected. The 'average' is a guideline only.
- Each child progresses at a different rate for each aspect of development. Your child might be able to play at a level expected for her age and yet may be able to talk only at a much younger age level.

Significant differences

Some differences in rates of development are worrying. Sometimes the gap in levels of development between a child and other children of her age does indicate a deeper problem. For instance, most children gain bladder control by the time they reach the age of three, and so parents are justified in seeking professional help if they find their child is still not toilet-trained by the time she is five. However, rarely does one particularly slow aspect of development on its own indicate a severe problem. A child with a significant development difficulty is often slow in more than one area. In most instances there needs to be a combination of several delayed features before more substantial investigation by a qualified professional is needed.

Determining the significance of delay in developmental progress is not always clear cut. Consider the following two children, both aged nineteen months:

Sue: She cannot walk yet, and most people would typically expect a child to be walking independently before that time. Closer investigation reveals that she appears to be thriving in all other aspects. She has started to put two words together to make phrases, she is a very active and alert child, she takes an interest in all that goes on around her, and she tries very hard to pull herself up on her feet using the coffee-table as a prop. Sue sees other children at her mother-and-toddler group who can walk, and she desperately wants to copy them.

Leslie: Like Sue, she cannot walk yet, and is unable to move herself round a room. Closer investigation reveals that other areas of the girl's progress are also impaired. Leslie makes very few sounds, and those that she does make are unintelligible babbles. Her concentration is extremely poor, which means she will not settle at anything for more than a few seconds. Toys slip out of her hands very easily, as if she does not have adequate control over any of her finger movements. Leslie makes no attempt to walk or pull herself up. She sits about passively all day, making no attempt to shift her position.

Both these children are lagging behind in their expected rate of physical development. Do you think the lag in development is significant for both these children? Do you think it is too early to say? Do you think one child has a more serious developmental problem than the other? By looking at the children's overall development it is clear that although ostensibly both have the same rate of physical development, there are vast differences between them. Sue is progressing well and is showing all the signs of wanting to be mobile: she will be able to walk very soon. Leslie's development shows all-round delay. Her slowness in walking is only one of several worrying aspects of her development.

Checklists of development

Psychologists, paediatricians and other child-care workers have devised many different sets of measuring scales for assessing progress in childhood, for example, the Children's Developmental Progress Charts, and the Portage Guide to Early Education. Some scales, such as the Bailey Scales of Infant Development, can only be administered by qualified psychologists. The compilers of the Griffiths Mental Development Scales even require that experienced child psychologists and paediatricians undergo further specialized training before being allowed to use the scales.

Despite apparent differences, developmental scales tend to have considerable overlap with many similar items. The developmental checklists given in this chapter – like some of the other checklists mentioned – focus on five key areas of child development:

- *gross motor development*. This is the child's physical skill which she acquires as she grows older. It includes the extent to which the child can co-ordinate her limbs, the extent to which she can move her body in a controlled way, and the extent to which she has good balance.
- *visual–motor development*. This is the ability to co-ordinate eye and hand movements and includes the extent to which

a child can pick up and hold small objects, the extent to which she can use hand implements, and the extent to which she can control a pencil when drawing or writing.
- *language development.* This is not just the rate at which a child acquires an extensive vocabulary of words. There is receptive language (the degree to which a child can understand what is being said to her) and expressive language (the degree to which she can use language to express her feelings and wishes). In virtually all children, receptive language proceeds at a faster rate than expressive language – normally a child can understand more than she can say.
- *social and emotional development.* This is the child's ability to interact with other children and adults. It also includes the level of the child's independence in basic self-care tasks, such as feeding, dressing and toilet-training.
- *intellectual development.* The best definition of intelligence is that it is the ability that allows a child to make sense of what is going on around her, the ability to adapt to, and cope with, new experiences and the ability to find a solution to novel experiences.

Remember that although each of these categories in the developmental checklist is presented independently of the others, areas of development interact. For instance, a child with limited language ability will experience difficulties when trying to relate to other children because she cannot communicate with them. This in turn might affect her gross motor development because she does not have as many opportunities to play athletic games as other children do. Similarly, an infant who is unable to sit up on her own will have difficulty in reaching for her toys, which in turn can affect her intellectual development because she is unable to explore her environment adequately. Therefore, when using the developmental checklist with your child, don't consider any category in isolation.

An accurate assessment

Psychological measurement is not straightforward. An assessment can be likened to a snapshot. And the psychologist assessing the child must be sure that the snapshot gives him a true picture of the child, that it does not catch her in an untypical posture. Consider the following:

Danny is four years old. At home he is very outgoing. He takes an interest in all that goes on around him and he talks fluently. Danny is an active child, who enjoys playing with a wide variety of toys. However, outside the family home Danny seems a shy child, afraid of new situations. When he is faced with unfamiliar faces he becomes clinging and uncommunicative. At a four-year developmental assessment, Danny was overawed by the strange surroundings. Due to this shyness, he acted immaturely and was unenthusiastic about everything he was shown. He would not perform any of the tasks that children his age are usually capable of completing.

The conclusion reached on the basis of that assessment was that Danny was not progressing as well as he should be. But his parents knew he was a completely different child at home. Who do you think is correct in the assessment of Danny? Are the parents right in thinking that he performed badly because he was shy of his surroundings? Is the professional right in thinking Danny has difficulties? They are probably both right in their own ways.

Equally important, do not look at a child's strengths and weaknesses in isolation from her background. A child at the age of five may be expected to be able to cut with scissors, but if she has never had the opportunity to hold a pair of scissors before, then of course she will not have mastered that skill. That is why a child psychologist will always consider as much additional information as possible when evaluating a child's progress. Only when all the different pieces of data about a child are put together can valid conclusions be reached.

Why developmental checklists?

For psychologists, developmental assessment is used to identify a child's strengths and weaknesses in order that areas of difficulty or delay can be targeted for some form of help. Assessment for its own sake is pointless. It is only justified when it leads to a positive course of action.

Fortunately, there is a wide range of help that can be given to children with developmental difficulties, though much depends on the individual needs of the child and also on the professional services available locally. Help for young children includes:

- *home visiting teaching*, to encourage specific aspects of the child's development, such as language and communication skills, or visual–motor co-ordination. The home visiting teacher usually calls on the child and her parents at home once a week or once a fortnight, for about an hour. In between visits, she will leave toys and activities for the parents to work on with their child.
- *admission to the local nursery*. In many cases, a child's developmental problem can be eased by mixing with other children her own age. Nursery placement has this advantage as well as providing the child with individual help should she require it.
- *admission to a specialist nursery*. Some children have a significant difficulty which prevents them from being able to benefit from attending their local nursery. A special nursery has more staff, who are specially trained, and fewer children. This allows each child in the special nursery to have as much individual attention as is necessary.
- *physiotherapy*, to encourage a child's physical progress. Physiotherapists will work with a child, usually once a week, at a clinic, in a hospital, in a special school, or in the child's home.
- *speech therapy*, to encourage a child's language development. Speech therapists usually work in a clinic or school. Sessions are usually weekly, lasting about thirty minutes.

Of course, in many cases developmental assessment reveals that there is nothing wrong with the child's rate of progress, that in fact she is developing normally. The positive use of assessment in that situation is to reassure the child's parents that all is well. Every psychologist would prefer to interview anxious parents and their child rather than having them sit at home worrying about her progress. Even when the assessment confirms progress is satisfactory, parents usually learn a lot about their child because they have been involved throughout the assessment process.

As a parent, you will find the following checklists useful in gaining a deeper understanding of your child's progress. The checklists and the accompanying information in this chapter will also give you an insight into the techniques and perspectives used by child psychologists when assessing the significance or non-significance of a child's development.

Development at three months

Gross Motor Development

- The baby has some head control at this age, whether lying on his back or face down. His head no longer flops about like a rag doll if not held securely by an adult who lifts him.

- Take a three-month-old baby and lie him on his back in a comfortable blanket. Once he is relaxed and contented in that position, take his hands in yours as if to lift him to you. You will probably find that he starts to lift his head off the blanket in anticipation of being sat up, even though he cannot sit up by himself yet.

- The baby's vigorous kicking movements become more co-ordinated. Limbs move more in synchrony than they did before.

- Back firmness increases and the baby shows some signs of straightening his back when sitting on your knee.

Developmental Checklists

Visual–Motor Development

- He is now able to use his eyes to follow an object as it moves round the room. The baby can also follow a moving toy as it goes up and down, or from side to side, or even as it goes round in a circle.

- Being more alert, the baby will show an interest in any human face that happens to be in the vicinity.

- The beginnings of hand control emerge. The child may suddenly bring his two hands together, almost as if he is not sure how he managed to do this.

- Familiar feeding objects, whether the breast or the bottle, will produce a reaction of anticipation whereby the child will thrust out his hands in the general direction of the food source as if trying to reach for it.

Language Development

- Whereas a young baby will be startled by sudden noises, the three-month-old infant behaves less erratically in response to noises. On hearing a small sound, such as a bell gently ringing, the child will become quiet and actually listen to it.

- Although the child cannot move his head towards a sound source, he may shift his eyes slowly from side to side in search of it.

- Parents often report that at this age the child likes listening to music, whether on the radio or sung directly to him.

- The child is usually able to make at least two distinct sounds, such as 'goo' or 'la'. This is the start of language as a means of communication.

Social and Emotional Development

- The first smile will have been shown at around the sixth

- Feeding becomes a tremendous source of emotional – as well as physical – nourishment. The three-month-old baby begins to focus on his parent's face during feeding.

- The baby enjoys company and familiar situations. He may smile when he realizes that bathtime has arrived.

- Many children of this age will keep their eyes on an adult walking round the room, especially if the adult is talking to them. The child is capable of making a distinct social response to a friendly person.

Intellectual Development

- An early sign of intellectual development is the baby's ability to see a link between his actions and a desired result. Gently place a clean tissue over a baby's face when he is lying on his back. He will make very general physical movements in a bold attempt to dislodge it.

- When a small toy is placed in his hand, his fingers will close round it, at least for a couple of seconds.

- The baby at this age shows fascination with his hands. He will wiggle his fingers, fan the air with them, or bring his hands up to his mouth to chew.

Development at six months

Gross Motor Development

- The child gains greater control over her limbs. When placed face down on the floor she will be able to lift her head, shoulders and chest off the surface, pushing with her hands to help.

- When lying on her back she will grasp adult hands as support to pull her head and shoulders up.

Developmental Checklists

- By six months most children are able to sit up on their own without any support, though they will occasionally topple over. When sitting up, the child holds her head firmly and may even turn her head round if something catches her attention.

- As well as being able to roll from side to side, she may begin to show the first signs of crawling. Place your child face down on the floor and put an attractive toy just beyond her reach. The six-month-old child will probably try to move towards the toy, perhaps drawing one knee up.

- Improved leg strength is also seen. Hold the child under her arms, in a standing position on a hard surface. She will take her weight on her outstretched legs and may even bounce up and down in excitement.

Visual–Motor Development

- The child now is able to keep her eyes on a toy that falls from her hands as long as the toy stays within her visual field. She will appear alert and interested, using her vision to explore her environment.

- She has better control over her finger movements. Rather than sticking rattles in her mouth as she did when she was younger, the child begins to use her toys more purposefully. She will shake them, rattle them or bang them deliberately in order to make a noise.

- Let the child fix you in his vision and then walk slowly round the room. The six-month-old child will watch you as you move from one side to the other.

Language Development

- The child can now detect a sound source more accurately, irrespective of which side the sound is coming from.

- She will enjoy listening to music. You will probably find

that music causes a change of mood so that the child stops crying when she hears it, or she may start cooing to herself.

- Babbling sounds are consistent, and when you are present your child may synchronize her speech with yours, rather like taking turns in a conversation. This delights both participants.
- The child can usually produce at least four different babbling sounds, such as 'aa', 'goo', 'eh', 'da', and so on.
- Speech becomes more closely linked to communication of feelings. The child may scream when she is annoyed or chuckle when she is playing happily.

Social and Emotional Development

- The child shows positive signs that she enjoys playing with a familiar adult, perhaps smiling or laughing occasionally. If you come towards your child, as if to lift her up, she will become excited in anticipation.
- There might be the first signs of shyness in the presence of an unfamiliar adult, particularly if neither parent is with her.
- The child likes to keep any toy that she holds. If you try to remove it from her, even playfully, she may grip it even more tightly. Most small toys end up in the child's mouth, after she has passed them from one hand to the other.

Intellectual Development

- The child uses physical movements more purposefully. Instead of trying to dislodge a paper tissue placed over her face by shaking her body, she will now simply pull it away.
- The child will now be able to hold a small toy in each hand without dropping either of them.
- She wants to get actively involved with her surroundings. Place a rattle just outside your child's reach. Instead of

sitting and staring at it, she will reach out to grab it. Similarly, when she is sitting in her high-chair, if you put a few small toys on the tray she will touch them almost immediately.

Development at nine months

Gross Motor Development

- The child can confidently sit up on his own on the floor, without any support, playing happily with the toys around him.

- Crawling is more co-ordinated. When the child is placed on the floor face down, with a desirable toy just out of his reach, he will make vigorous crawling movements in his attempts to reach it. Both knees are drawn up and his arms might be stretched out, although he still cannot get the object.

- He may show his first stepping response. Hold your child under the arms and let him take his weight on his feet. You will find he puts one foot ahead of the other.

- You may find that your child is able to stand up when gripping on to a low table or chair for support.

Visual–Motor Development

- When sitting in his pram, if the child accidentally – or deliberately – drops a toy, he will peer over in the appropriate direction, looking for it.

- Place a small piece of biscuit on his high-chair tray, and you will see the child use his thumb and forefinger to bring it up to his mouth, rather like a pincer movement.

- The child is aware of the link between his hand and eye movements. Tie a small toy on to a piece of string. Having attracted your child's attention to the toy, demonstrate how you can get the toy to come towards you by pulling the string. Then put the string into his hand. He is likely to imitate your action.

Language Development

- The child is able to use his hearing to pinpoint accurately a sound source. If you bring a ticking watch up to his ear without his seeing it, the child will immediately turn his head round to see what is making the noise. You should get the same reaction when you say his name.

- The infant will be using two syllable babbles, for example, 'agah', 'eleh', regularly.

- The first word may appear at this age – it is usually 'mama' or 'dada'. The excited parental reaction on hearing this first 'real' word from the child acts as encouragement for him to say it again and again.

Social and Emotional Development

- The child can tell a stranger from a familiar person, and signs of shyness are obvious.

- Negative emotions can be expressed clearly. Try taking a toy away when he is playing with it – he will make a big fuss.

- During feeding, the child gets involved by trying to hold the spoon, or perhaps wrapping his hands round the drinking cup. Of course, he cannot yet manage these utensils on his own but he does make an effort.

- The child begins to initiate social relationships. He may pass his toy to the awaiting hands of a friendly adult, even though he usually drops it.

- Hold a mirror up to the child's face. The alert child will smile at his own reflection or try to touch it. He is aware there is something in the mirror.

Intellectual Development

- If the child is holding one small toy in each hand and then you pass him a third, he will probably drop one of the toys in order to accommodate the one being offered to him.

- He will have started to play with two toys together, for example a plastic cup and saucer, or two small threading cubes.

- Children of this age love crumpling up paper – so keep that important letter away from him or you will see it twisted playfully in your child's enquiring hand.

- The child now sees associations between events where he did not see them before. Let your child watch you place a sweet under a cup, right in front of him. He will lift the cup up straightaway because he knows the sweet is there.

Development at one year

Gross Motor Development

- A child at one year is usually well able to crawl around the floor on her hands and knees. However, some children prefer to 'bottom shuffle' about the room instead.

- She is steadier on her legs now and may be able to walk around furniture, for example, a settee, by holding on to it firmly and side-stepping her way round. If your child uses a play pen regularly, you will see her use the upright bars in this way.

- For many children – but not all – the early signs of independent walking are there. Take your child's hands while she is standing up and gently coax her forward. You may find she takes some hesitant steps forward, using you as support.

Visual–Motor Development

- At one year, the child grips an object in a mature way, fully able to co-ordinate her thumb and forefinger in a pincer-type grip.

- Place an interesting toy or sweet just out of her reach and she will probably use her index finger to point directly at it.

- Some children start to use a pencil or crayon properly by trying to make some mark on the paper instead of simply putting it in their mouths.

- There is great interest in every movement in the environment. Roll a small toy car across the floor in front of your child. You will see her reach across for it, pick it up, and then play with it.

Language Development

- The child can use at least three clear words to describe familiar objects. And she uses these words appropriately, in the correct context.

- She will be able to follow basic directions. If you ask your child to give you a toy, or perhaps to wave goodbye to you, her correct response will confirm she understands what is required.

- Hearing is sharp at this age, but if the sound is repetitive then the child will lose interest quickly.

- The child will also talk away to herself when on her own or when engrossed in some play activity.

Social and Emotional Development

- At this age, social interaction interests the child. She enjoys playing very elementary games, such as pat-a-cake, with an older child or adult. You might even find that your child waves bye-bye to you without any prompting.

- She likes to give – and receive – affectionate embraces with those adults she knows well.

Developmental Checklists

- The child likes to get involved with her own feeding and dressing. For instance, you may find that when you start to put her jumper on she puts her arms out in anticipation.

- She can hold a cup and drink out of it with only a little help from you.

- Objects are used constructively in play. Give your child a plastic cup, saucer and spoon from her doll's tea set and you will see she plays with them appropriately. The spoon may be placed in the cup or perhaps the cup rested on the saucer.

Intellectual Development

- Many children at this age can imitate adult actions. Show your child how you can bang two small wooden bricks together to make a loud noise. Then hand her two bricks of her own. She will probably copy you.

- While she is holding one brick in each hand, pass her a third. You will find she can hold all three without dropping any.

- The child is fascinated by any object that rattles, and will want to know more about it. Put a couple of wooden beads into a small cardboard box, rattle it, then hand it to her. She is likely to open the box in order to find out what is inside. This interest in simple puzzles is a positive sign of good intellectual development.

Development at fifteen months

Gross Motor Development

- By this age most children are tottering about – albeit rather shakily. (Bear in mind that some normal children do not walk until beyond this age.)

- A child at this stage of development loves pushing wheeled toys about the house or in the street (under supervision).

Understanding Children

This activity boosts his self-confidence and feelings of independence.

- The child may be able to kneel on his own on a chair while at the table, or perhaps on the floor while playing with toys.

- Take your eyes off your child for a moment, and when you next turn round the child is halfway up the stairs – crying because he is not sure how to get back down again.

Visual–Motor Development

- The child will have established a preference for one hand over the other, and the grip in that hand is mature.

- Take two small objects in each of your own hands and put them into the child's hands, two objects in each. By fifteen months you may well find the child holds all four successfully – if only for a few seconds – before dropping them.

- Children of this age enjoy playing with moving objects. Roll a small ball towards the child and watch as he gleefully attempts to reach it, or perhaps hit it away. If the toy is out of his reach and he cannot toddle about yet, then he is likely to point furiously at it.

Language Development

- The infant likes rhymes and songs. He may try to join in if he hears you singing, and familiar rhymes like 'Round and round the garden' or 'Knock on the door' will be greeted with delight, as he anticipates what comes next.

- Although the fifteen-month-old child cannot say his own name he may recognize it when someone else uses it. In the child's presence, talk to another adult. When he is looking away, introduce his name into your conversation without giving it particular emphasis. Watch carefully to see if he turns round in recognition.

- The child can use at least three or four clear words in their correct context, and he will understand a lot more.

- Simple commands, such as 'Leave it alone' or 'Get your juice' should get an appropriate response from the child.

Social and Emotional Development

- The child is more co-operative now, keen to help in his basic management. When dressing him, you will find he tries to help by perhaps putting his arms out in anticipation, or getting his own slippers.

- This desire to get involved extends to feeding as well. The child should be able to use a spoon for feeding himself, although some of the contents may get spilled in the process. With your help, he might be able to hold a cup and drink from it.

- Exploration is the name of the game at fifteen months. Constant supervision is needed as the child's inquiring mind takes him into all sorts of interesting – but possibly hazardous – parts of the house. Ordinary household items become transformed into toys as the child rattles, for example, a packet of dog food to discover what sort of noise it makes.

- The child's tendency to put everything into his mouth decreases.

Intellectual Development

- Boxes of any size seem to have an inherent fascination for children of this age. Take a small box that has a lid, let the child see you place a couple of small toys inside, and then hand the closed box to him. At first he may just rattle it, but eventually he will remove the lid and get the toys out. He may even do this if you hand him two boxes at once. The more mature child will put the toys back in the box if requested.

- You can start to use elementary form boards at this age.

Understanding Children

Most good toy shops now sell form boards with only one or two shapes in them. If you demonstrate to the child how the shapes fit in the board, then he may be able to imitate your actions.

Development at eighteen months

Gross Motor Development

- At this stage, the child is usually able to walk comfortably and steadily on her own, and may even be able to trot about the room.

- Take a small toy over to her. Just as she reaches for it, let it drop on to the floor. The eighteen-month-old infant can bend down and pick up the toy without losing her balance.

- Climbing ability has improved. The child should be able to climb into a low armchair, and then turn round and sit back. If the chair is small enough, she can slide backwards into it.

- Children of this age thoroughly enjoy pulling toys on a string along with them as they trot up and down the house.

Visual–Motor Development

- Place a bundle of building bricks in front of the child and start to build a small tower, one brick on top of another. Encourage the child to imitate what you are doing. She will probably manage to build a tower of three bricks before it falls over.

- Pencil control is more mature. The child can scribble freely on paper.

- The child's interest in books is positive. She enjoys storytime and points out recognizable objects that appear in the pictures.

- Children of this age can see the link between their actions and the environment. Take one of the toddler's favourite toys and place it out of her reach at one end of a towel spread on the floor. Show her that pulling the towel will bring the toy towards her. She may well be able to imitate your action so as to acquire the object.

Language Development

- Vocabulary is now at least six clear words, although the child understands many more. She tends to prattle on using long babbled sentences, with some of the words intelligible.

- When the eighteen-month-old infant wants something, whether it is a glass of milk, or the television turned on, she will point at it, using some form of language to indicate her wish.

- When you speak directly to the child, she will listen to what you say. Ask her to pass you a familiar object, for example, a cup or a ball. Even though she may not be able to say the word herself, she will carry out the instruction properly.

Social and Emotional Development

- The desire for independence shows through. The child makes good effort to manage her own feeding. She can drink out of a cup without spilling much of the contents. The spoon consistently reaches her mouth, and very little falls on to the table in the process.

- Home becomes an environment to be explored. The toddler will make energetic attempts to open and shut doors. She can also take off her unfastened shoes and socks by herself.

- Despite this wish to do things on her own, a child at this stage of development can be very clinging to her mother and father at times.

- She enjoys imitating simple everyday actions, like washing the dishes, or cleaning the floor.

Intellectual Development

- Interest in form boards continues. The child can cope with more complex puzzles of this sort, with perhaps three or four pieces in them.

- Give the child a box with a couple of small bricks rattling inside it. Having emptied them out, she may be able to put the bricks back in the box and fit the lid on securely.

- The child's memory is sufficiently mature for her to be able to remember where certain objects, such as her cup, or her favourite toy, should go. This means she can find them when she wants and – hopefully – is able to put them away when she is finished.

Development at twenty-one months

Gross Motor Development

- The child climbs upstairs – and down again – without adult help.

- Motor skills are more advanced. He is steady on his feet and runs about comfortably without danger of falling over. The child may be able to jump from the floor so that both feet leave the ground at the same time.

- Some children at this age can walk upstairs independently. However, the child's lack of confidence may make him prefer to crawl upstairs on his hands and knees. But with a little parental encouragement he might do it properly.

- Getting into a small chair, at a table, is within the child's capability.

Visual–Motor Development

- Give the child a small rubber ball and ask him to throw it to you. You will find he makes a good attempt at this. Instead of simply letting the ball drop from his hands, he uses his wrist in a definite throwing movement – although the ball does not always go in the desired direction.

- When playing with toy building blocks, the child can build a steady tower of up to five bricks.
- Improved pencil control allows the child to scribble in a more co-ordinated way. He will be able to scribble using long straight lines, rather than the haphazard strokes he used previously.
- Take two cups, one empty and one with a small amount of water in it. Show the child how you can pour water from one cup into the other. The child should be able to imitate this, without spilling any of the contents.

Language Development

- Vocabulary is extended to at least twelve identifiable single words. And significantly, the child starts to combine them to form two-word phrases, such as 'Juice gone' or 'Daddy out'.
- The child can identify familiar objects if shown a picture of them. Let him look at a 'first picture book', where there is one picture to a page, for example, a dog, a house, a table, etc. He will be able to name at least one of them accurately.

Social and Emotional Development

- The child begins to develop an understanding of body parts. When shown a doll, he can point to one or two items when asked, such as hair, eyes, feet, nose, and so on.
- Some children aged twenty-one months have bladder control, but this depends greatly on the parents' attitude to toilet-training. Many parents prefer to leave this until slightly later.
- The child shows signs he wants to tell others about his daily experiences, and, although language is not well developed,

Understanding Children

he can communicate, for example, that he saw his favourite programme on television, or that his playmate took his toy away.

Intellectual Development

- The child can complete unfamiliar form boards without requiring much practice – as long as there are only three or four pieces to them.
- Memory continues to improve and he can reliably find familiar items in the house, without being told where they are.
- Many children of this age become engrossed in imitating whatever their parents are doing in the house. Previously, the child would only do this for a short time, but now involvement in this activity is sustained.

Development at two years

Gross Motor Development

- Using a wall or banister as support, the child walks up and downstairs on her own, though she still puts both feet on the one step before moving up or down to the next.
- Being steady on her feet, the child can walk or run up to a ball and kick it without falling over.
- A child of this age enjoys sitting on a tricycle, or indeed on any pedal toy. Although she cannot use the pedals to propel the toy, she moves it along the floor by pushing with her feet.
- A two-year-old is usually able to throw a small ball in a definite direction while remaining upright.

Visual–Motor Development

- The child can now build a steady tower of at least six or seven blocks.

Developmental Checklists

- Because her pencil grip is more mature – she holds the pencil towards the tip, using the thumb and first two fingers – the child can make a reasonable attempt to copy a vertical line.

- She is able to pick up very small objects with ease. Give the toddler a small wrapped sweet and you will find she unwraps it without difficulty.

- By two years of age, most children have established a definite preference for using one hand or the other. If the child is given one of her favourite story books, she will be able to turn the pages over, one at a time.

Language Development

- Vocabulary is at least twenty or thirty words, and the child understands a lot more. She talks in short sentences, putting two or more words together to make a meaningful phrase.

- The child listens to what is said to her and she attends to any general conversation that is going on around her. When playing on her own, the child often talks continuously to herself, but if you eavesdrop you may not understand what she is talking about.

- She loves nursery rhymes and songs at this age.

- When asked to identify certain body parts, the toddler can reliably indicate hair, eyes, nose, mouth, and feet.

- Two-year-olds often seem obsessed by the names of people and objects, and constantly ask parents what something or someone is called.

Social and Emotional Development

- The child can open and close doors by herself. However, she does not have full appreciation of routine hazards so you have to be very careful when she goes out of your sight.

Understanding Children

- Tantrums often emerge at this age – hence the description 'the terrible-twos' – and this arises out of the child's frustration when she cannot get what she wants. The child may appear very stubborn, determined and demanding, especially when her parents show momentary interest in another child.

- Toilet-training is usually well under way by the end of the second year, and many children are reliably dry during the day.

- The child is a more independent eater now. She can lift up a filled cup from the table, take a drink and put it back. She can spoon-feed herself without dropping the food all over the place.

Intellectual Development

- Take a set of plastic toy barrels, the sort where the barrels vary in size and fit inside one another. Select the smallest barrel, unscrew it, and let the child see you put a small toy in it. Then screw the barrel together – not too tightly – hand it to the child and ask her to get the sweet out. Many two-year-olds do this successfully, but it is not easy.

- The child's increasing ability to solve new situations means she can cope with jigsaws and form boards of greater complexity.

- By two years of age, the child is often ready to play with doll's house furniture and doll's house people, using them appropriately.

- The child may also refer to herself by her proper name.

Development at two and a half years

Gross Motor Development

- The child's physical skills are increasing. He can now balance on his tiptoes although he can only hold this position for a few seconds.

Developmental Checklists

- He makes reasonable attempts at jumping. With both feet together, he can push himself off the ground.

- Stairs are no longer the obstacle they used to be. The child is confident and capable enough to walk upstairs and downstairs again without your help. However, he will want to hold on to a rail or banister for support.

- If he has a toy wheelbarrow, or any large movable toy like that, he will be able to steer it along the ground without bumping into too many objects along the way.

Visual–Motor Development

- Picture books interest the child of this age. He will take great delight in spotting the small details in the pictures and pointing them out to you.

- Hand preference is firmly established by now. The child will hold a pencil confidently, probably gripping it with three or four fingers, but steadily enough to make a mark on a piece of paper.

- Bead threading is an activity that will attract the child's attention. However, he will have great difficulty in threading a lace through the hole in the bead unless both the bead and the hole are large enough.

Language Development

- Pronouns come into the child's vocabulary for the first time. Words like 'me', 'I', and 'him' become a regular feature of the child's speech.

- He constantly asks questions about everything that he sees or hears. Don't give him detailed answers, but instead keep your replies at an elementary level.

- By now he has a wide range of words in his vocabulary. The child will probably be able to use well over a hundred words in their proper context.

- Most children of this age are able to tell someone their first name when asked by another child or adult.

Social and Emotional Development

- Although the child is probably fully toilet-trained during the day, he may struggle to pull his pants and trousers back up after using the toilet. He should be able to pull them down by himself.

- Tantrums continue throughout this stage. In fact, you may find they are becoming more frequent and stronger as the child's temper continues to feature prominently.

- Feeding habits have become more composed. He may experiment with his food but in general he will make good attempts to eat tidily.

- The child does not join in full co-operative play yet. He enjoys being in the presence of other children but will tend to keep himself to himself for the moment. He is not keen to share his toys or possessions with anyone else.

Intellectual Development

- When shown coins, the child of this age will probably be able to say that they are money. However, he will not be able to identify individual coins.

- Show him a photograph of himself, on his own, without you in the picture beside him. He will probably recognize himself.

- Draw a straight line across a blank piece of paper while your child is watching you. Then hand him the pencil and ask him to copy it. He will make a good attempt to do this, although the line will not be as straight and as steady as yours.

Developmental Checklists

Development at three years

Gross Motor Development

- The child will be able to walk upstairs, like an adult, putting one foot on one stair then the other foot on the next stair. Coming down, she still puts both feet on the one stair before descending on to the next one.

- Ask your child to stand on the second bottom step in a set of stairs. Stand beside her and let her watch you jump off with both feet together. She probably can do this as well. If she is not confident enough to try this from the second bottom step, then try her from the bottom step itself.

- She can stand on her tiptoes and at the same time she can walk several paces without upsetting her balance.

- Large play apparatus such as a slide, balancing log, or swing, will interest her. Some of these toys will be beyond her but she wants to try anyway.

Visual–Motor Development

- At this age, using small wooden building bricks, the child can build a tower of at least eight bricks before it falls over.

- She will begin to grip scissors properly. If you let her use a pair of child's scissors, with their specially shaped handles, she may be able to cut up pieces of paper.

- Pencil control is improving. Let her see you drawing a circle. She will make a recognizable attempt when copying you. Similarly, she will enjoy painting pictures as long as the paint brush is large enough for her to grip comfortably.

- The child is more capable at threading a lace through beads, and no longer requires very large beads for this.

Understanding Children

Language Development

- The child talks confidently in three- or four-word sentences.

- The number of 'who', 'what', 'when', 'how' and 'why' questions increases as her thirst for knowledge of the world around her increases.

- Stories provide a considerable source of enjoyment. She will have her favourites which she asks to be read over and over again.

- Her language becomes more elaborate. Perhaps for the first time, the child begins to use adjectives in her conversation. At this stage, she probably has only two or three descriptive words but she uses them properly.

Social and Emotional Development

- The child has greater control over the use of cutlery during mealtimes. She is able to use a spoon and a fork together to feed herself, without any help.

- Many children of this age have bowel and bladder control throughout the night as well as throughout the day.

- She can dress and undress herself as long as the fasteners are not too small or complicated. The child can possibly manage to undo large buttons, but she is unlikely to be able to fasten them.

- Fantasy play is very popular at this age. Give your child some of your old clothes to dress up in, and you will find she is able to amuse herself for several minutes as she acts out various imaginary roles when dressed up.

Intellectual Development

- The child is able to make elementary comparisons of size. Give her a large glass of juice and a small glass of juice,

Developmental Checklists

and ask her to point to the big glass. She will probably be able to make the distinction without much difficulty.

- She can cope with larger form boards now, perhaps with up to seven or eight pieces in them. The child will also be able to manage a two-piece or three-piece jigsaw.

- At this age, you may see the first signs of colour recognition. Your child will not, as yet, be able to identify all the primary colours by name, but she will probably be able to match two items of the same colour, especially if they are red or yellow.

- Ask your child to draw a picture of you. As well as putting in your head, she may draw in your legs or your arms.

Development at four years

Gross Motor Development

- He can use pedals properly to propel a pedal car or tricycle along the ground.

- The child enjoys energetic outdoor play. He will take great delight in trying to master climbing frames, balancing logs, trampolines and swings.

- Balance is sound. You will find that your child can undertake a variety of physical tasks successfully, such as hopping a few paces on one foot, walking steadily along a straight line, and travelling up and down stairs, one foot in front of the other, without any help.

- The child enjoys participation in ball games. Kicking, catching and throwing skills are all more advanced at this age.

Visual–Motor Development

- Cutting is more mature. Now, when using scissors, the child can cut a sheet of paper into two relatively similar-sized pieces.

Understanding Children

- The child's drawing of you is more identifiable and contains more details, such as eyes, hair, hands, or mouth, than his drawings did when he was younger.

- He enjoys bead-threading, and can cope with a thinner piece of thread and smaller beads.

- Give your child some crayons and a blank sheet of paper. Ask him to draw a picture of his house. Although details will be missing, you will see that his drawing is recognizable.

- The child can pick up very small items, for example, a piece of thread, or a pin, without much difficulty.

Language Development

- The child's language is completely intelligible. He has a broad vocabulary, with an ample use of personal pronouns and adjectives.

- He is able to give an accurate account of relatively recent experiences at home and in nursery.

- Colour recognition is more firmly established. The child may be confident enough to identify two or three colours.

- Nursery rhymes and songs are very popular.

- The child begins to develop a sense of humour. However, sometimes he will laugh at a joke simply because he likes the sound of the words, not because he really understands what the joke is about.

Social and Emotional Development

- The child can dress and undress himself without your help, apart from small buttons, buckles and zip fastenings.

- By this age, he has begun to play co-operatively with other children. He accepts the need to share, and to take turns. The child can quickly lose his temper when playing but is less likely to storm off in a huff.

Developmental Checklists

- He will be able to give the correct response to 'How old are you?' or 'What is your age?'
- The child takes an interest in helping around the house. He will probably want to help you, especially when it comes to setting the table for a meal. If asked, he will be able to set out cutlery in approximately the correct places.

Intellectual Development

- He can complete jigsaws with up to fifteen or twenty pieces in them, although he may require your encouragement if he finds them difficult.
- The child will have the first stages of counting. He may be able to recite the numbers up to ten, or even beyond. Place four of the same objects, for instance, sweets, and ask the child to count them out, pointing to each one as he does so. He may be able to do this accurately.
- Basic comparisons are within the child's grasp at this age. He will probably be able to differentiate successfully between two objects when deciding which one is larger/smaller, heavier/lighter, taller/shorter, and so on.
- Some children at this stage are able to give their full name and address when asked.

Development at five years

Gross Motor Development

- The five-year-old is agile, and is able to engage competently in various physical activities such as running, jumping, climbing and kicking.
- She is totally independent on the stairs, going up and down without any help at all. The child is also able to run upstairs without falling over.
- Other physical skills, involving balance, should be well

developed. You will find that your child can hop several paces on one foot, and that she can skip from foot to foot.

- Ask your child to bend and touch her toes without bending her knees. She will probably be able to do this, although she might require some practice before mastering it.

Visual–Motor Development

- The child can cut accurately with scissors.

- Some children at this age are able to make an identifiable attempt at writing one or two letters, usually the ones that appear in their names.

- Drawing skills are more mature now. Many children are able to draw a recognizable house, with windows and doors in it, and a recognizable man, with arms, legs, and hands. Pencil or crayon control is better, allowing the child to colour in shapes more neatly than before, without straying over the outline.

- Show the child some simple shapes and ask her to copy them. She should be able to do this without much difficulty.

Language Development

- At this age, the child is usually able to speak quite clearly and has little difficulty in making herself understood by unfamiliar adults.

- She shows a keen interest in language, and language activities, such as story-telling, nursery rhymes and song, and even jokes. The child may also like singing advertising jingles that she has heard on the television or radio.

- Many five-year-old children are able to state their first name, their last name, and their address, when asked.

- When asked a direct question, the child will be able to give a sensible and relevant reply. She will be able to follow simple instructions.

Developmental Checklists

Social and Emotional Development

- The child is able to eat properly using a knife and fork, assuming she has child-sized cutlery.

- Independence skills are well established. The child usually can dress and undress herself without help, can tidy away her toys and clothes when asked to do so, and can look after her basic cleanliness (as long as you keep reminding her).

- When playing with younger children, she will take a somewhat protective attitude towards them. The child will try to comfort other children her own age or younger if she sees they are crying.

- Co-operative play is in evidence. She can mix well with other children, being able to participate in a game that has rules. Dressing-up play is very popular at this age.

- She should be able to separate well from you when being left at nursery or primary school.

Intellectual Development

- The child probably is able to count up to seven, or beyond.

- She will have an idea about the different time phases of the average day, and will know that breakfast comes before lunch, that dinner comes at the end of the day, and so on.

- Take one of each coin and ask your child to name them. She may be able to identify two or three coins.

- Jigsaws usually do not present much of a problem, as long as they have interesting pictures and around twenty pieces each.

- The child can match most colours and is able to name three or four colours confidently.

Index

age gap, 58-8, 81
aggression, 50-6
   discipline, 53-4
   'dos' and 'don'ts', 54-6
   inborn, 50-1
   social influences, 51
   television, 51-2
   see also fighting
attention-seeking behaviour
   reasons, 38-9
   strategies for overcoming, 39-41

Bailey Scales of Infant
   Development, 178
bed-wetting, 25, 111-13
   see also toilet-training
behaviourism, 14-16, 23
birth order
   balancing the effects of, 82-3
   factors influencing, 81-2
   first-born, 73-5
   only children, 80-1
   second-born, 76-7
   twins, 77-80
   youngest, 77
bonding, 32-7
   breast feeding versus bottle
     feeding, 33
   factors affecting, 34-5
   lack of, 37
   takes time, 32-4
Braid, 11

bullying, 157-8

Children's Developmental
   Progress Charts, 178
chromosomes, 4
comforters, 43-9
   dummies, 46-7
   excessive use of, 47-9
   positive aspects, 49
   reasons for, 43-4
   see also masturbation; thumb-sucking
crying baby, 35-8
custody and access, *see* divorce

deafness, *see* hearing difficulties
development
   individual differences in, 24, 176-8
   phases in, 24
developmental checklists, 176-209
   accurate use, 180
   purpose, 181-2
   types, 178-9
   three months-five years, 182-209
discipline
   'dos' and 'don'ts', 161-4
   reasons for, 159
   when to start, 160
   see also aggression; self-image; spoiling